P9-CFS-367

HONEY, BABY, MINE

HONEY, BABY, MINE

A Mother and Daughter Talk
Life, Death, Love (and Banana Pudding)

LAURA DERN & DIANE LADD

Foreword by
REESE WITHERSPOON

GRAND
CENTRAL

NEW YORK   BOSTON

Copyright © 2023 by Laura Dern and Diane Ladd

Cover design by Elizabeth Connor
Cover photo of authors courtesy MGM Media Licensing
Cover copyright © 2023 by Hachette Book Group, Inc.

Hachette Book Group supports the right to free expression and the value of copyright. The purpose of copyright is to encourage writers and artists to produce the creative works that enrich our culture.

The scanning, uploading, and distribution of this book without permission is a theft of the authors' intellectual property. If you would like permission to use material from the book (other than for review purposes), please contact permissions@hbgusa.com. Thank you for your support of the authors' rights.

Grand Central Publishing
Hachette Book Group
1290 Avenue of the Americas, New York, NY 10104
grandcentralpublishing.com
twitter.com/grandcentralpub

First Edition: April 2023

Grand Central Publishing is a division of Hachette Book Group, Inc. The Grand Central Publishing name and logo is a trademark of Hachette Book Group, Inc.

The publisher is not responsible for websites (or their content) that are not owned by the publisher.

Grand Central Publishing books may be purchased in bulk for business, educational, or promotional use. For information, please contact your local bookseller or the Hachette Book Group Special Markets Department at special.markets@hbgusa.com.

Photo credits are listed on page 237.

Print book interior design by Gabriele Wilson

Library of Congress Cataloging-in-Publication Data
Names: Dern, Laura, author. | Witherspoon, Reese, writer of foreword.
    Title: Honey, baby, mine / Laura Dern and Diane Ladd ; foreword by Reese Witherspoon.
Description: First edition. | New York : Grand Central Publishing, 2023.
Identifiers: LCCN 2022053106 | ISBN 9781538720370 (hardcover) |
    ISBN 9781538710210 | ISBN 9781538720356 (ebook)
Subjects: LCSH: Ladd, Diane—Family. | Dern, Laura. | Actors—United States—
    Biography. | Cancer—Patients—United States—Biography. | Mothers and
    daughters—United States—Biography.
Classification: LCC PN2287.L135 D47 2023 | DDC 791.4302/80922
    [B]—dc23/eng/20221127
LC record available at https://lccn.loc.gov/2022053106

ISBN: 9781538720370 (hardcover), 9781538720356 (ebook), 9781538710210 (large print), 9781538757536 (signed edition), 9781538757543 (special signed edition), 9781538757680 (special signed edition)

Printed in the United States of America

LSC-C

Printing 1, 2023

"Life is an unanswered question,
but let's still believe in the dignity
and importance of the question."

—TENNESSEE WILLIAMS, *WHERE I LIVE: SELECTED ESSAYS*

ALSO BY DIANE LADD

Spiraling Through the School of Life:
A Mental, Physical, and Spiritual Discovery

A Bad Afternoon for a Piece of Cake:
A Collection of Ten Short Stories

Contents

HONEY, BABY, MINE

For mothers and daughters, fathers and sons—

and for any two people willing

to tell each other the truth,

or at least to boldly ask the questions.

Foreword

BY REESE WITHERSPOON

The first time I met Diane Ladd—the woman I had admired since I saw her in *Alice Doesn't Live Here Anymore*—she was seated in a screening room on the 20th Century Fox lot, about to watch the film *Wild*.

Laura Dern—Diane's daughter, my mother in the film—and I had decided it would be a good idea to show the movie to our parents early so that they could prepare themselves. The intensely emotional story is based on the memoir by Cheryl Strayed about how she walked a thousand miles of the Pacific Crest Trail to recover from the devastating loss of her mother.

There is a sort of immediate intimacy that happens when people play family members in a movie. It's hard to describe the process that actors go through—losing all inhibitions as fast as possible and falling in love or building a relationship in a matter of weeks. In the case of Laura and me, it took an hour. The first day of shooting, we filmed her death scene in a musty, dilapidated hospital. I threw my body on top of hers and wept while she dutifully kept her eyes sealed. The moment Jean-Marc Vallée yelled, "Cut!" we burst into laughter over the absurdity of our job.

During that shoot and the publicity tour that followed, Dern (I call her Dern) and I shared so much: Our childhood dreams of being actors. Our love of acting and all the films that inspired us. Our mutual friends. Our families. To say that she has become a dear friend would be an understatement. We consider ourselves sisters. If ever there were a process to make this legal, we would be there with documents in hand, ready to pledge allegiance to each other.

I'd gotten to know her two incredible children (with her ex-husband, the musician Ben Harper)—Ellery, age twenty, and Jaya, age sixteen. So the natural next step was to meet each other's mothers—which brings us back to the 20th Century Fox lot, sitting down with these women who'd raised us and watching them watch us model some of the very life lessons they'd taught us.

Our mothers held hands during the whole film. At the end, they sat staring at the screen and crying quietly together for a long while.

Laura and I did too.

We all went to lunch afterward, and it was the beginning of a magical friendship.

I have come to call Diane "my other mother." Her voice, a low Mississippi drawl, reminds me of lightning bugs and sweet tea and bourbon. The way she carries herself so elegantly through rooms and dresses for every occasion and always has endless genuine and effusive compliments for people she loves—and sharp words for those she doesn't—to me makes her the embodiment of southern grace and charm. And I've never witnessed a better storyteller in my life.

She's one my very favorite actors because of her ability to show a spectrum of human emotion with such authenticity. She can explore the depths of despair, break your heart into a million pieces, or tell the bawdiest joke—sometimes all in the same scene. She brought her incredible talent to the films *Chinatown*, *Ghosts of Mississippi*, and *The Cemetery Club*, and she was deservedly nominated by the Academy for her roles in *Wild at Heart*, *Alice Doesn't Live Here Anymore*, and *Rambling Rose*. Not to mention her wonderful stage and television work. What a joy it was to see her and Laura play mother and daughter on the phenomenal HBO show *Enlightened*! *Time* magazine once said Diane "is one of the top ten actresses not only in this country but the whole world." I could not agree more. She is the stuff legends are made of.

As for Laura—how do you describe a force of nature? She is a hurricane of creativity and intelligence, passion and humor. A gale-force wind of ferocious love. A tidal wave of questions and curiosity. She's always ready to push an idea further out on a ledge, create necessary chaos, shake up stagnant rooms, *wake everyone up!*

Growing up, Laura learned from her extraordinary parents how to use pathos and humor to create indelible characters. Her father is Bruce Dern, one of the most prolific and respected actors of his generation—known, of course, for his iconic roles in *Coming Home* and *The Great Gatsby*, and as the only actor ever given the honor of killing John Wayne in a movie. In the myriad important films her parents made, she saw them directed by Martin Scorsese, Mike Nichols, Roman Polanski, Hal Ashby, John Frankenheimer, and Alfred Hitchcock. Family friends included Shelley Winters, Jack Nicholson, and Dennis Hopper.

Laura was nominated alongside her mother for an Oscar for her performance in *Rambling Rose*. She went on to deliver stellar performances in *Wild at Heart* and *Citizen Ruth*, both essential viewing for any aspiring actors. She gave Marmee boundless warmth in *Little Women* and divorce lawyer Nora Fanshaw profound ruthlessness in *Marriage Story*. But my favorite of her performances has got to be as the social-climbing alpha female Renata Klein in *Big Little Lie*s, probably because I had a front-row seat to watch the magic happen.

Off-screen, too, she just *cares*. A whole lot. About people in this world, about relationships and communities. She cares about art and self-expression. On a set, she's like a child on the playground imagining the most elaborate game of make-believe, and you get to play it with her.

Every time I see her soar into her rightful place as the talented, brilliant woman she is, I'm overwhelmed with emotion and pride for my friend whose body of work is so singular and impactful. On Oscar night 2020, I sat at home in my PJ's shrieking with joy and snapping photos of my TV every time I spotted her on the red carpet. And when she won the Best Supporting Actress Oscar and dedicated it to her mom and dad, I burst into tears.

I knew that sharing this historic Hollywood moment would be so important to them because of the many nominations they had received from the Academy, separately and, in the case of *Rambling Rose*, together. Knowing their love of the industry and the respect they have for their peers, I was deeply moved to see their family's legacy cemented onstage that night. As far as I'm concerned, it remains one of the best Oscar moments ever.

Around that time, as her career reached a new pinnacle, Laura told me that her mother's health had taken a dramatic turn. A lung condition had made it hard for her to breathe. The doctors said she might have only a few months left to live. I was so moved when Laura told me that they'd begun taking walks every

DIANE, REESE, LAURA, AND BETTY—SUNDAY BRUNCH

day to help her mother heal—and when she added that they'd begun taping the conversations they had during those walks to preserve Diane's stories for posterity.

In every mother-daughter relationship, there are memories that deserve time to be explored and reexamined through a different lens. We grow up. Our parents become vulnerable. How we handle these times is a true mark of our character. Knowing them both, I was not surprised to hear that in the conversations they were tackling trauma, joy, love, death, and every other topic, and that the walks were healing not just physically, but also emotionally and spiritually.

Neither of these women ever takes one moment for granted. They ponder life's biggest questions fearlessly, always aware of how precious and fleeting our days can be. I have watched them argue and reconcile. I have watched them fall into a tender embrace after dinner. I have sat at their feet and learned from them— two of the most fabulous, glorious, talented women alive.

Now that they've decided to share these walk-and-talks—along with gorgeous family photos, tasty recipes, and reflections on so much that they've experienced separately and together—you get to join them as well.

Laura

The doctor visit started routine and turned serious. Tests. More tests. Then sitting there and learning that my only-child mother who had raised only-child me, my constant companion, the person I rely on more than any other, will not be a permanent fixture in my life. We know we don't get each other for the whole ride. It's still shocking when your mother reaches her stop.

The doctor gave her a time limit. *Six months*. Hearing those words, I felt the walls crumbling around me. I lost my footing. Nothing made sense. *But she's so strong! I thought. Impermeable! The hardest worker I know. She's never not working. Or writing. Or organizing. Or helping. Or fixing. Or reading and trying to learn more. And now her body is demanding she stop.*

I have no answers. And I am proud of how well I can solve problems and break down walls. But maybe I can't fix this.

I looked at my mother sitting beside me in that doctor's office. She seemed, suddenly, so frail and so uncertain. My eyes filled with tears. As I gazed at her, I thought: *You can't die. You are too alive. You, my constant, have all these delicious qualities that no one else I know embodies. I need you to live.*

The doctor gave me only one thing to hold on to. He said it might help her oxygen levels if I could get her to walk a bit, expand her lung capacity. How could I make walking joyful when even a few steps exhausted her? I had to eliminate the prescription component and turn it into a creative challenge for my storyteller mom. To commit herself to healing, my mother would need to feel that this was an artistic job. She'd been cast as someone who walks, someone who recovers. Hmmm . . .

As if in a Santa Monica version of *The Arabian Nights*, it became my job to keep her talking (and therefore walking) as long as possible. Just as Scheherazade delays her own death night after night by keeping the king entertained, so I hoped that our telling these stories would extend my mother's life. I thought: *These walks might be our final moments together. The only way I can cope with my fear of her dying is by making sure that we talk about everything and that we leave nothing unsaid.*

In the months that followed, we talked through happy memories and old wounds—some of which healed as a result of these conversations. I became closer to my mother than I ever had been before. I learned things about her I'd never known and discovered another side to stories from my childhood. I pushed her to walk farther than she thought possible and to talk honestly about even the most painful things—her divorce from my father and a family tragedy that occurred before I was born and overshadowed my childhood, the death of my parents' first child.

We are sharing these intimate conversations here now in the hope that they will be inspiring to others. We're also including photographs, recipes, and reflections to pay tribute to all the things that make up our life together.

I thought I was doing all this walking and reminiscing for my mother's sake, to give her peace and strength in her final months or years and to let her know how she'd shaped me and how grateful I was for her example. But I would come to learn that this time with her was a gift for me as well.

Back in that doctor's office, I didn't know yet that any of that would happen. When we began, I was just a scared daughter ready to do whatever it took to keep her mother alive. And so when we heard the prognosis, I turned and said, "Mom, it's time we told each other everything. We deserve to know each other truly. Let's walk tomorrow, and every day after until you are better. I will record our talks and we will have this forever—our story, saved on these recordings, committed to the page."

"YOU, MY CONSTANT, HAVE ALL

THESE DELICIOUS QUALITIES

THAT NO ONE ELSE I KNOW EMBODIES.

I NEED YOU TO LIVE."

DIANE AND LAURA, *WILD AT HEART*

WALK

1

THE FAMILY
BUSINESS

LAURA: OK, Mom, here we go. A great parking spot, look how lucky we are! I know you're breathing heavy, but you can do this. Let's get out of the car and then just do half a block, OK?

DIANE: [*Wheezing.*] I can't do it. I can't do it.

LAURA: Mom, how about just a few minutes? I'm here to lean on. Hey, tell me a story.

DIANE: A story? I'm about to drop dead, and you want a story?

LAURA: Yes! OK, let's get out and cross over to the walking path and start talking.

DIANE: Drive me across the street first.

LAURA: Mom, it's literally eleven steps across the street.

DIANE: Laura, it's so far from us.

LAURA: We're not going to drive to the other side of the street. We're parked. Let's go!

DIANE: It was already thirty steps to get to the car. Across the street, then on the sidewalk, and it's— [*Gasps.*]

LAURA: Just remember, the doctor said with every step your lungs are expanding, you're getting more oxygen, you're getting better, and you'll get back on the set. OK? That's our goal.

DIANE: Right. That's our goal.

LAURA: And this isn't just from your daughter; this is someone who knows that no matter how you feel, the minute you start acting, you're suddenly cured of all ailments. But we have to get you strong enough to get back to that. And we can do it. Just give me fifteen minutes a day, OK?

DIANE: Are you sure?

LAURA: Yes, I'm sure.

DIANE: That doctor said I'd be dead in six months. And he didn't even tell me. He took you aside and told you. The coward. [*Long pause, walking in silence.*] Do you believe him?

LAURA: I believe he's very smart about certain things, but I believe he's wrong about your prognosis. What were *you* thinking when you heard that?

DIANE: What do you think? It's terrifying.

LAURA: For me too, Mom. Let's prove him wrong, OK? I know you love life and you love being an actor. And you've got a lot more to say and do, so let's keep walking. From now on, we are no longer going to listen to what anybody believes will happen in six months. What we're going to do is be here in this moment together and do what we know we can to heal you, which is getting oxygen into your lungs. One step at a time, and we're just going to talk, right?

DIANE: All right, Dr. Dern. Let me hold on to your arm. You've at least played a doctor on film, haven't you?

LAURA: Only in *Jurassic Park*. But a pretend paleobotanist is practically a real pulmonologist, right?

DIANE: Uh...

LAURA: Maybe you shouldn't listen to me. But I'm going to make you walk anyway.

DIANE: Fine. I'm going to pretend this street is water and I've got Jesus's ability to walk on it. OK?

LAURA: If that's what you need to cross the street.

DIANE: Yeah. Hold my arm tight, Saint Peter.

LAURA: Whatever it takes.

DIANE: I've tried to walk on water many times in my life. I think I've been lucky to make it through a few mud puddles. [*Breathes hard.*] This hurts, Laura.

LAURA: Mom, I thought a natural place to start talking would be working together. I've been thinking a lot about what a gift it's been to work alongside you all these years at a job we both love. I mean, many people follow in their parents' footsteps and do the same job, but they don't usually work side by side. How lucky are we?

DIANE: I've always said that it's a gift when parents get to work with their children. Oh, remember that hat shop in New Orleans?

LAURA: Yeah, I do. We saw the mother and daughter working on hats together.

DIANE: Every feather, every pearl, every bauble was just so! And one time I was at a butcher shop and the butcher said, bursting with pride, "That's my son helping me."

I think a lot of parents want their children to go into the same business. I didn't want you to go into the business.

LAURA: What are you talking about? Yes, you did. You were delighted when I booked jobs as a kid.

DIANE: No, Laura.

LAURA: What were you most worried about?

DIANE: My God in heaven, Laura! The rejection! The unsteadiness of it! Never knowing when your next job will come—if there will even be another one. But I had to let you, because of your talent. And because you outsmarted me. You met a film agent at a party and said, "My mom and daddy won't help me, and I want to act!"

LAURA: Yeah, I was ten. We were at your friend Bo Hopkins's house. His agent was there. I knew she worked with children also and was very patient and seemed very kind. You guys had just finished the movie you made with Johnny and June Carter Cash. And so it felt familiar enough for me to hang out with you all and go up to his agent and say, "My parents don't want to help me. Would you ever let me audition for you to see if you thought you would send me out on an audition or two to get feedback?" I didn't know about doing contrasting monologues or any of that. So I did a children's poem called "The Little Peach" by Eugene Field. To show her my range, I did it in seven different, well-practiced—and in retrospect completely ridiculous—accents. She eventually sent me out on a few auditions and you seemed okay with that.

DIANE: I was always proud of your work. But I was afraid for you.

LAURA: Why?

DIANE: Why! As if you don't know. I wanted to protect you! It's a hard, hard business. [*Coughing fit.*]

LAURA: Remember to breathe. Let's get the pulse oximeter out. I think your oxygen level just went down.

DIANE: I've got to sit down, Laura. I've got to sit down, right here on the bench.

LAURA: No. Wait, Mom.

DIANE: Come on, let's go sit down. Look at the—

LAURA: I'll tell you what, before you sit down, let's just take two relaxed deep breaths...so that we can talk more about the stress of the movie business. [*Laughs.*]

DIANE: If I sit down, I'll be able to take that deep breath. I can't take that deep breath if you won't let me sit down. I've got to sit.

LAURA: Do you see that bench? It's about ten feet ahead of us and it's a better view of the water. Do you see it?

DIANE: Oh boy, pin a rose on me, that's far. Do I get a lollipop like at the doctor's if I have to do all that? 'Cause you're starting to piss me off.

LAURA: Yes, Mom. A lollipop or a sticker or a cocktail, whatever you like. Before we sit, take a deep breath. Because once we sit, we can take a nice long break. Deal?

DIANE: OK. But you talk for a minute while I catch my breath. What's new with Ellery and Jaya?

LAURA: Oh, I'm about to freak you out. Ellery had coffee yesterday with David Lynch, and David gave him a DVD of *Wild at Heart*.

DIANE: He did?!

LAURA: Apparently Ellery's been watching all his movies, and he said to David, "I can't find *Wild at Heart* anywhere." So David gave him the DVD, but when he did, he said, "Wait to watch this one until you're thirty." And Ellery said, "Why? Is my mom crazy in it?" And he said, "It's not you seeing your mom I'm worried about. It's you seeing your grandmother that might be worth the wait."

DIANE: [*Laughs.*] Hilarious! He's not wrong. Were you worried about Ellery watching it?

LAURA: Oh, I forbade him from watching it! I might show him a few scenes, especially one that's a particularly special memory I have of working with you. Can you guess what scene I mean?

DIANE: The one in the police station?

LAURA: Yes, where Sailor is locked up and I'm crying on the bench.

DIANE: Before the scene we were on opposite sides of the set doing our different preparations. You knew even then that you have to build that wall between you

DIANE IN *WILD AT HEART*

and the crew and your other actors so you are alone in the scene. Then they started shooting, and I came in and said, "Oh, honey baby!" We sat on that lonely bench in that police station and we both cried together. Sobbed! You were using your own private memory. I was using mine. At the end of the scene we looked up and into each other's faces. You knew what I was thinking about. You could feel it. And as I looked into your eyes, I knew what you were feeling.

LAURA: That was crazy. I was seeing *you* there at the same time that I was seeing your character. I saw you and I thought, *Here is the woman who knows me better than anyone.* There was no acting in that moment. I was just a daughter reacting to her mother. That's one of my favorite moments as an actress, getting to be in that scene with you.

DIANE: But that moment—when we looked in each other's eyes—it was like we saw each other standing there naked with everyone else clothed. We witnessed each other's vulnerability. And do you remember what happened?

LAURA: We started laughing.

DIANE: We burst out laughing, like kids getting the giggles in church!

LAURA: When your job is to tell the truth, and the person you're working with knows you really well, they're going to know if it's bullshit. You can't cheat and you can't escape. And we were so lucky to not only have our own artistic bond but to have someone like David Lynch who felt like family and allowed us to be part of his work. Here's a question for you: Why would we be muses to David Lynch and not someone like John Hughes?

DIANE: Ha, I guess he just suits us better? Or sees us in a specific way?

LAURA: Even before we all became such good friends, he knew how to read both our needs in one moment. After *Wild at Heart* wrapped, remember you and Martha Coolidge gave me a birthday party at her house? My twenty-first birthday. I can't remember—was it a surprise party?

DIANE: Yes, it was. A beautiful, wonderful party. Sweet Martha outdid herself. She had a ton of food and a horse for people to ride because her home bordered a ranch.

LAURA: It was a small group. I remember "the other Diane Ladd" was there, aka Diane Lane. Everyone confuses your names. David brought me to set me up for the surprise. My amazing girlfriends were there: Bellina Logan, Moon Zappa, Brooke Shields, Mandy Foreman. And when you brought my birthday cake out with my face on it, David was able to compliment you on the cake while acknowledging my trauma. I think he said something like, "Diane Ladd, that cake is the most creative way to make sure your daughter is unstable enough to want to play interesting women for the rest of her life!" And I said, "Meaning you've just traumatized your daughter into a lifelong path of therapy and art."

DIANE: I thought it was a magical caring thought to have your beautiful face on top of your cake! I had to go to a different city to get it done!

LAURA: Well, thank you I guess?! But still traumatizing…And man, David knows us both so well…Do you remember the premiere of *Wild at Heart*?

LAURA AND NICOLAS CAGE IN *WILD AT HEART*

DIANE: Yes, that's when you and Nicolas Cage were into wearing matching outfits. You showed up that night in those matching Richard Tyler suits in burgundy satin. He had a men's suit and you had that micromini.

LAURA: Oh, I loved that outfit. That was such a special movie for us, but when it came out, we were so nervous about Grandma seeing it! David even said at the premiere, "Oh, Mary's here?" and seemed curious how she'd take it. We were all wondering the same thing: How would this five-foot-one Alabama Catholic grandmother respond to this radical movie in which her daughter and granddaughter are pretty boundary-less?

DIANE: Yes, and then as soon as the movie finished, do you remember what she said?

LAURA: Yep. She went right up to David and said, "Ooh, I loved it! That movie was so *cute*! And Nicolas sings just like Elvis!"

DIANE: That's right! We all looked at each other like, *Cute? What movie did she just see?* [*Coughs.*]

LAURA: Just take a nice, relaxed breath. You've got your oxygen helping you. Good.

DIANE: I really want to sit down, Laura.

LAURA: Of course, but let's just go to the next bench and then I'll hold you like you held me in *Enlightened* when I was having a panic attack.

DIANE: Oh, that did feel special!

LAURA: Yes, remember? I was sitting on a bed. Luke Wilson's character had come back from rehab with a letter for me. And I'd just started the thing with Dermot Mulroney's character, the *Los Angeles Times* journalist. Todd Haynes, our director, put you and me alone in a room to just be together quietly with the camera, and he kept the crew out. And of course we kept a bit of that show with us. I'm thinking of Ginger.

DIANE: Oh, I loved that dog! Ginger had the soul of a human!

LAURA: Don't you think it's a little weird that you adopted her off that set, Mom?

DIANE: What are you talking about? She was retiring from show business. I had to take her in!

LAURA: But in the show, the dog is my nemesis. Every time I had a scene with the dog, I was saying things like, "Shut up, Ginger," or "Fuck you, Ginger." And the dog

GINGER IN *ENLIGHTENED*

was trained to bark whenever I came into the room. Does that really seem like a good pet for you?

DIANE: Laura, the grandkids made me adopt her! But I guess she was scared of you for a while.

LAURA: Yeah, I screamed at her for two years on the show! And you adopted her with this built-in knowledge that she was going to hate me!

DIANE: Well, she did get over that eventually. Wait, what time is it? You've hypnotized me, Laura! And now I'm coming out of it. I'm so tired.

LAURA: We can turn around and walk back now. How are you feeling about your lungs? Are you able to believe you're getting better?

DIANE: Here's the really good thing, honey: There was no doctor in my head today because I was busy talking to you. There was no trouble with my lungs because I was busy listening to my daughter. But I can't walk this much every day. I can't do it, honey. My lungs hurt so much now.

LAURA: Well, they're sore because you're pushing oxygen in there. And that's a good thing. You're pushing through scar tissue, but you're also getting healthier with every step, and you have to trust that. Day by day, it'll work. You'll see.

Laura

How grateful I am that Mom and I have gotten the chance to work together. The first time was in David Lynch's 1990 movie *Wild at Heart*, in which we played a mother and daughter.

David had been my primary mentor since I was seventeen. The casting director on his movie *Blue Velvet* knew me from a few things by that point, so I got a call asking me to meet with David. He doesn't do traditional auditions, preferring to go on instinct, so he invited Kyle MacLachlan and me for lunch to get a sense of the two of us together. We'd never met before. We went to Bob's Big Boy and shared french fries. We wound up doing the movie together and later became a couple.

Kyle, David, and I spent a lot of time together having dinners and hanging out. David is such a visionary and such a meticulous artist. In addition to being a genius, he is also the kindest person. Mom often joined us for these meals, and they became close too.

When he read *Wild at Heart*, the Barry Gifford novel, David called me saying he wanted me to play Lula and Mom to play Marietta. I was so excited. The first scene Mom and I shot for *Wild at Heart* was one in which I came down the stairs and Mom pointed a finger at me to warn me off of my boyfriend, Sailor, played by Nicolas Cage. She said, "Don't you dare talk to that boy again!"

Well, I burst out laughing and wrecked the take. I was twenty-two, and I'd had that same finger wagging at me my whole life!

Mom started laughing and then so did the crew. They all knew, I think, how hilarious it was for us to be acting out this insane version of our relationship. In the film I even hallucinate her flying on a broomstick alongside my car dressed as the Wicked Witch from *The Wizard of Oz*. Let me tell you, it's a crazy thing when you see your mother dressed as the Wicked Witch of the West. That's like twenty years of therapy in an hour.

People sometimes imagine that playing this extreme, antagonistic mother and daughter would be stressful, but filming with her was a total joy. The weirder it got, the more fun it was. That's all thanks to David, who has become my best male friend. He and I call each other "the Tidbit." He started calling me that when we were doing *Blue Velvet*. When I asked him what it meant, he said, "You know! A little bit of *tid*! A little something special!"

One day on the set of *Wild at Heart*, while my mom was getting her Wicked Witch makeup put on, Nicolas Cage came over to me and pointed to her and said, "Look over there. That's your *mom*."

I said, "I *know*."

DAVID, BELLINA, DIANE, AND LAURA

"People sometimes imagine that playing this extreme, antagonistic mother and daughter would be stressful, but filming with her was a total joy. The weirder it got, the more fun it was."

—LAURA

Diane

As we made our first drive up to the Palisades bluffs in Santa Monica for a walk, I kept looking over at Laura in the driver's seat. She looked so determined.

When it comes to these walks, I can tell she means business. I want to go along with her plan, but I'm scared, and I can't let her know it.

I'm also furious that I'm sick. My doctor, I, and many people in my town believe that my condition is due to industrial farming in my area. They were spraying in my neighborhood with pesticides—like we were cockroaches! For three years! Without telling me! Over ten pesticides were being sprayed, including glyphosate—which can cause all sorts of terrible things! It was only after my dog, Ginger, was poisoned by the air and died in my arms that I began to realize what was happening. I was left with lungs so severely damaged that I can barely breathe.

I went to one doctor after another, and no one gave me the right answers.

Are you sure you're not a smoker? they asked, looking at my scans.

For one year, decades ago, I smoked. That's it.

I was given one misdiagnosis after another: vertigo from an inner-ear infection, an esophageal disorder . . . finally they called it idiopathic pulmonary fibrosis, IPF. And they confirmed to me that the pesticides were the cause. Such bad scarring in a nonsmoker almost always comes from environmental toxins.

Now I can't stop gasping. And Laura is going to make me *exercise*? The pulmonary specialist—another of these fancy doctors who know everything and talk about me like I'm not there—told Laura, "Even if she only walks half a block, that will make a difference. It's about getting the lungs to work harder for fifteen minutes a day. Don't let her stop before fifteen minutes, whatever it takes."

Fifteen minutes? Fifteen seconds feels impossible. I have oxygen going into my nose through a cannula. The doctor said I might be hooked up to this machine for the rest of my life. Terrifying.

But what upsets me most is Laura seeing how weak I am. That day at the doctor's office when we got the news, she broke down. She said, "But I still need you, Mom. You can't leave me." Now all I can think is that on one of these walks, I'm going to fall down dead on the sidewalk. I picture Laura having to call an ambulance, standing over my body as a crowd gathers. How can I walk as much as she wants me to when I'm terrified of dying in front of her?

The pain from my lung scarring is incredible. My esophagus has shrunk and I'm starving. People bring soup, mashed potatoes, milkshakes, but whatever I can get down isn't enough. I wake up at four thirty in the morning, staring at the ceiling—depressed, exhausted, hungry, hurting. I'm sure that Laura dragging me out into the sunshine is the right thing, but it's hard in every way.

I don't want to think about dying. So many questions keep going through my head: *What if I'm not around to see my grandchildren grow up? What if I'm not there when they need me? Will I miss their heartbreaks, their marriages, their babies? Will I never get to experience the joy of watching them find their way in the world?*

What keeps me going is that desperate longing to do more. I worry that I didn't hold my loved ones enough, that I didn't ask the right questions or give the right answers. I imagine myself in a coffin, pounding on the lid, saying, "Wait! Just one more week, one more day, one more minute! Don't bring the curtain down yet!"

LAURA'S 6TH BIRTHDAY

"Diane Ladd, that cake is the most creative way to make sure your daughter is unstable enough to want to play interesting women for the rest of her life."

—LAURA, QUOTING DAVID LYNCH

WALK

2

TIME TOCK

DIANE: Guess what? I got offered a job today. A Hallmark Channel show called *Chesapeake Shores*. I want to take it, but how am I going to work with a cannula in my nose? How will I know if I'll be strong enough by the time they start shooting?

LAURA: Mom, this is another reason we're going to get you strong. If we get you walking, we'll get you off that cannula. And if you still need it sometimes, maybe they'll write it in.

DIANE: I sure hope so.

LAURA: You're looking very fit today!

DIANE: Oh no. Does that mean you're going to make me walk extra far?

LAURA: No, we'll do our fifteen minutes, and then it's up to you how much more we do, OK?

DIANE: Deal.

LAURA: Wait, your shoelace is untied.

DIANE: You don't need to do that, Laura. I can tie my own shoe.

LAURA: Just let me do it. How many times have you tied my shoes?

DIANE: [*smiling*] You cute thing.

LAURA: Here's something I've always wondered about: How did *your* parents feel about *you* being an actress? Now think about it, don't answer instantly. Because all I've ever gotten from you is, "Oh my God, they loved it!" Knowing them, I just can't believe that. What was that first conversation? Did you sit them down and say, "I want to be an actress," and they said, "Cool"?

DIANE: Hardly. They thought it was cute until they realized I wanted to do it for a living. I did my first real, non-Christmas-pageant play in high school.

LAURA: What was it?

DIANE: A one-act called *The Grand Cham's Diamond*.

LAURA: What is that?

DIANE: An English play by Allan Monkhouse about a stolen diamond. It's set in a London apartment. I didn't want to be the young lead, Miss Perkins. I wanted the part of the older woman, Mrs. Perkins. That was a part with a little depth. And I got it as a freshman in high school. I remember being onstage and looking out at the audience and realizing that everybody in that theater, all those people, walk around daily with some kind of mask hiding most of their feelings in life! Sitting there in the dark, they felt, for a moment in time, somehow secure. That mask was lowered! I could *feel* it! That's why plays and movies are so important to me. Nobody's looking at themselves or their neighbors or judging them. They're watching what's going on right in front of them—just energy flowing toward and around them, and they can relax.

LAURA: That's lovely, Mom.

DIANE: While standing on that stage, as I looked out into that audience, I felt like I could reach out and touch every single human being, and that I *knew* each and every one. It was a mystical experience. When I laughed, they laughed. When I cried, they cried. It was as if I was not one body, but one with all! I still feel that feeling whenever I'm acting. And over time I learned that you can't make a bad play great, but you can make it bearable. And you can make a good play much better, and you can make a great play really appreciated. If you connect to that audience, it's living energy. So when I step on the stage, it feels like an opportunity for healing. It's as if my soul takes over. The personality is not driving the car anymore; the soul is. I'm in the creative flow, doing my work. But my parents didn't see all that. They just said, "My kid's doing a play. She's good in it." They enjoyed that part, sharing the achievement.

LAURA: It's hard for me to imagine you doing anything else besides performing. Once they realized how serious you were about being an actress, did your parents support your dreams?

DIANE: They didn't exactly get me dancing lessons. My mother bought me a hope chest. You know what that is?

LAURA: Isn't that the chest that you keep things in, and then it's given to your husband or something?

DIANE: Sort of. It's for the woman to have lots of pretty things stored away in waiting for her wedding. I guess it's your parents' way of saying, "Sure hope you get married!"

LAURA: *Vomit.*

DIANE: The chest contains blankets, sheets—

LAURA: Condoms?

DIANE: *Nooo.* Lace doilies for your furniture, napkins, linens—

LAURA: You never gave me that stuff. Maybe that's why my marriage ultimately didn't last. It's your fault. *[Laughs.]*

DIANE: A hope chest was like a dowry. It was typical of the time in our part of the South. My mother had that darn hope chest right at the foot of my bed as a constant reminder.

LAURA: Yuck. Doesn't it send the message that girls are worthless, so they have to come with stuff? "Please marry my daughter. I'll give you some nice sheets if you take her off my hands!"

DIANE: I agree with you, but it's tradition.

LAURA: It's a disgusting tradition.

DIANE: Well, we were a typical middle-class family, but one wealthy relative, Aunt Marguerite, was very politically connected and even held a position in the government, and I was her favorite niece. She wanted me to live with her, be a debutante in Mobile. She made sure I had some pretty little organdy dresses. I guess to help with that goal, did you know that in 1951, my family put me in a finishing school? Boy, that almost finished me.

LAURA: Wait, why?

DIANE: The diction teacher had a worse accent than me. You had to pick up a pencil with your lips and roll it with your tongue! Maybe that's how I became a great kisser! With a pencil in my mouth, I had to say, "Hello. How are you?" No wonder I can project! If I'm onstage in front of five thousand people, that last row can hear me without my having to yell! But it's a wonder I didn't get lead poisoning. I hated that place so much. I walked around with a book on my head all day, and they took away my organdy dresses and gave me tailored suits. They wanted me to shave off my eyebrows and draw them on. And they gave me that awful bra that you had to pump up with air. You'd go out to dinner, feel it leaking, have to go in the bathroom, take a straw, and blow up your bust.

LAURA: Oh my God, everything about this story is terrifying. A blow-up bra? Gross! And you have great boobs!

DIANE: Not big enough ones for the Jane Russell era. I was thin. I had a great body, but small boobs. Those inflatable bras were crazy, though. One girl from our school got on a plane, and the cabin pressure made her bra explode.

LAURA: Oh my God! That reminds me of when Shelley Winters made me stuff my bra for my first play audition. It was with her for *The Effect of Gamma Rays on Man-*

in-the-Moon Marigolds. While we were doing the audition, she decided the director couldn't see enough of my face because my hair was in the way. So she grabbed the bow attached to my blouse to tie my hair back, not realizing that the string was holding the shirt together. In front of the director, my blouse came off and there I stood onstage in my bra with tissue pouring out of it.

DIANE: Oh my God in heaven! You poor girl! I remember your saying at that young age, "After this experience with Shelley, *no audition* will ever frighten me!"

LAURA: But back to your finishing school.

DIANE: Yes, it was really not a good school, OK? And I quit at sixteen, walked out without telling my parents and got a job at a bank in New Orleans.

LAURA: Mom, you were a baby!

DIANE: So was one of my favorite saints, Joan of Arc. She left at sixteen just like me, and she had a little voice that talked to her, just like me! But that's right, Laura. It was a miracle I didn't encounter more danger. At that age, we'd go down to the Latin Quarter and we'd dance with all the foreign exchange students. I became a great dancer: tango, mambo, everything. It feels like a long time ago. I'm feeling a little bit winded. Why don't you talk for a minute so I can catch my breath? Remember when Bruce's family, the blue-book aristocrats, wanted you to be a debutante? You went to New York and were staying with your aunt Averil.

LAURA: I love that you call her my aunt, even though she was your best friend.

DIANE: True, because she was like a sister, and how great that her daughter Bellina became your best friend and my godchild.

LAURA: Dad's family had let you know that the debutante ball was going to be held that week I was in town. Our family was in the social registry, whatever that is.

DIANE: That's Grace Kelly time!

LAURA: *[continues]* You offered to get me a beautiful gown and...

DIANE: *[interrupting again]* AND A CHAPERONE! I had promised Bruce's mother that I would let you do that!

LAURA: *[continuing again]* I *told* you I wanted to check out the scene *first*, and so I went to a reception the day before the ball to see what it was all about. In my charcoal-gray pantsuit, I walked into a room with a bit too much of the color white.

I felt really uncomfortable at the lack of diversity and the lack of authenticity. All the girls were in fluffy party dresses. I didn't disrespect their choices. I just felt no connection to it. A chaperone asked me why I was leaving when she saw me walking out. I said, "I forgot my pearls."

DIANE: Ha! I remember that you called me that night and said, "These are not our people."

LAURA: Yes.

DIANE: But then you did not come directly home.

LAURA: No. Some friends and I joined the model United Nations. It was supercool. I loved that experience.

DIANE: Well, I wanted my daughter to use her wings to learn how to fly.

LAURA: But wait, you still need to tell me how your parents reacted to you wanting to be an actress as a career. You said they were fine with you acting until they realized it wasn't just a hobby.

DIANE: It was actually pretty bad. This one night, Mother was really—I mean really, really—upset. She'd had a bad argument with my dad or something. Trying to cheer her up, I said, "Mother, it's all right. I'm going to be an actress, and when I get famous, I'm going to buy you a beautiful home and make everything OK!" She turned on me and said, "You stop that talk right now, young lady. You're never going to be an actress! You live here in the South. How in God's name, Diane Ladner, are you going to be an actress? Why, daughter child, you're thinking plumb crazy! You can't go running off to Hollywood or New York or somewhere. This talk about you acting *as a career* is absolutely ridiculous, and I'm sick of it! I don't want to hear it anymore—and I mean it!" And she stormed out.

LAURA: That's awful. Do you think it's because she was frustrated? She'd wanted to be an artist herself, and if she couldn't do it, you couldn't either?

DIANE: Maybe. Mother was a terrific singer, but she didn't have the gumption to go for it! When people would say to her, "Oh, Mary, Diane's got a great voice," she'd nod, and then she'd start to hum a little bit, and then before you knew it, she was singing in full voice, to show what *she* could do. Whatever the reason why my mama said that about how I'd never be an actress, I was so shocked. Silly me, all that time, really I'd just thought she believed in me. So I prayed half the night. I couldn't sleep. I lay there looking out my window at the sky, and I cried and prayed to God: "You tell me. You don't want me to be an actor? OK. But I think I'm supposed to." I sobbed. I felt so lost. And I wrote a poem, "Time Tock." I still remember it to this day. Let me recite it for you.

Oh time, time, time,
> *don't tick to me!*
You fly like a witch through the night
> *though it be day.*
Ere it might bring good fortune when my hope screams,
> *"Yes!"*
I hear the sounds of you daring us . . . daring our trust . . .
No, no,
> *Yes, yes,*
>> *Maybe,*
>>> *So,*
So, I beg you. I plead, "Wait, wait, wait,"
> *and you run on, leaving us alone.*
In vain, I turn round and there you are . . . laughing,
> *or are you crying?*
You envelop, whispering in my brain,
> *while one screams, "Stay!"*
Please stay back. Do not follow us . . . for we are not sure . . .
> *We are filled with fear.*

"Come one, come all, To the Twenty-First Century Game"

Uncertainty and doubt wrestle with the remote-controlled soul
> *in her match against the world.*
We cannot afford the price of a ticket.
> *Faith is to be the referee,*
>> *for refreshments, unique indeed, a sip of water known as sweat.*
Many of us no longer know her taste in our mechanized vacuums.
> *We are not sure.*

I am not sure . . . of these I ask:
> *Let my heart love, and be worthy of that love.*
> *Let my hate be consumed to purify and protect*
>> *that love without benefit of destruction.*

> *Let me leave this earth having done one thing,*
>
> > *to make an as-of-yet-unborn child a better human being.*
>
> *I ask for:*
>
> > *A drop of wisdom,*
> >
> > *Then, to shed the tear of understanding,*
> >
> > *A sigh of that high-priced commodity, peace.*
>
> > *Give me but a laugh,*
> >
> > *A moment to smile a true smile,*
> >
> > *And I will ride with you, but first . . . first*

LAURA: My God, Mom! That poem is incredible! And your sixteen-year-old self wrote that? You were really crying out to be an artist.

DIANE: Yeah, but wait. Here's the thing: The next morning was Sunday. After praying all night for clarity, I went to church. Our little church never had guest speakers— I mean *never*—but that morning they did! And guess what his sermon was about? The gifts God gives us, and what we do with 'em! That guest speaker said, "Everybody has a different destiny. Some of you will stay where you are in life. Some of you may have to travel miles and miles away to complete your test! If you have a calling, you must answer it. It's God's will. If a man has seven gifts, he should use seven gifts. If he has one, he should use one. If you have to leave your mother, father, hometown, to use that gift, you have to. It's what God wants for you, or he would not have given you that gift."

LAURA: No!

DIANE: I swear to God, Laura. I thought, *God, you have answered my prayers!* I didn't know how I was going to do anything, where I was going to go. But I figured that if he could answer my prayers that fast, then I did not have to worry about it. I could be true to myself, put one foot in front of the other, listen and go forward, and he would surely show me the way. And indeed he did. Never said it would be easy, and it was not.

LAURA: And you didn't know any actors?

DIANE: I didn't know *anybody* who did anything creative.

LAURA: So at sixteen years old you're in New Orleans . . .

DIANE: Yes, and eventually by a twist of fate involving someone from out of town seeing a play I was in, I ended up getting an audition with John Carradine to step into the role of Pearl in *Tobacco Road* out in San Francisco. It was like—

LAURA: "The hand of God." You've told me that part of the story before.

DIANE: Well, it was! That's how I left the South. I was given a train ticket to California. So I was sixteen, twenty-five dollars in my pocket, on the Sunset Limited. It was my first trip out West on a train. There was only me and one other person in my car. The other person turned out to be Vice President Richard Nixon's mother. When she said goodbye, she said, "Be careful. People aren't as friendly out here as they are in the South, Diane!" She also told me to visit her, and I said to her, "I'm going to be an actress. I'll visit you when I'm a big star!"

DIANE AT 17

LAURA: Your parents let you do the play in California?

DIANE: They just figured I'd have a little quick adventure and I'd come back home. But after that I went to New York, and from then on I was working all the time, and so there was nothing they could say about it. By the time I was seventeen, I was doing *Orpheus Descending*, Tennessee Williams's modern retelling of the Orpheus myth, at a little theater in New York. We were told if we got the reviews, we could take it to Off Broadway. But the reviewers didn't come. The actors were all distraught. How could we get a good review if the reviewers don't come? I thought, *Why mess around? Let's start at the top*. I called up the *New York Times*. Don't ask me how I got the editor on the phone, but I did. He said, "Honey, we don't review Equity Library Theatre plays," like it was scum. I said, "What are you talking about? I'm an actress. What does it matter where I'm acting? If I'm an actress, I'm an actress. The only thing I have for all this work is a piece of paper that could be your review! Without it, it's all in vain! You've got to review it!" I started sobbing, and he sent a reviewer.

LAURA: And didn't Tennessee Williams himself come to see you in it?

DIANE: Yes, he sure did. I hadn't met him before, but I called and invited him. I said as my cousin he had to show up.

LAURA: I know you always say we're related, but how is that exactly?

DIANE: We're not close cousins, but we're cousins. His full name is Thomas Lanier Williams III. Our branch of the family changed Lanier to Ladner, and then when I got to Hollywood, I was told to shorten it to Ladd. Tennessee went by Tom. His sister was named Rose, like me.

LAURA: It's confusing when people go by their middle name like you do.

DIANE: It's very common in the South. Anyway, as people know, the character of Laura Wingfield in *The Glass Menagerie* was based on Tom's sister. When she was young, she was diagnosed with schizophrenia, and their parents had a lobotomy performed on her. It's a horrible tragedy. Tom told me that she liked little crystal animals and she liked to smoke. When Tom visited Laura, he would bring her Wings cigarettes. And he told me that when his family found out he was gay, they were going to have a lobotomy done on him too! They put him in an institution when he was about eighteen. But it so happened that there was a young intern there who was gay, and he left a window open and helped Tom jump through the window and run for his life. Thank *God*. Or we wouldn't have some of the best plays in American history.

LAURA: Amazing. And Dad was in that show?

DIANE: [*Chuckles.*] I'm getting there! We got this magnificent review, so now they let us take the play to Off Broadway. Tom took me under his wing then. I was supposed to star in a film he was doing, but the studio wouldn't have me because I was unknown, so they gave the part to Jane Fonda.

LAURA: You were born to be in Tennessee Williams plays. Pedro Almodóvar even said that at the Golden Globes. He found me while I was walking to the bathroom or whatever, and he said, "You have to take me to meet your mother!" So I walk Pedro over to meet you, and he bowed down and kissed your feet.

DIANE: I wish he'd give me a job! I loved the kisses, but—my God, to work with him!

LAURA: If anyone should work with Pedro, it's you. You and he would be a dream. But you'd have to speak Spanish. Do you remember he said to you, "You in *Wild at Heart* were my inspiration. No one has ever been like that but Tennessee Williams women!" And if you think about his movie *Women on the Verge of a Nervous Breakdown*, there is a kind of spirit of Blanche DuBois! You don't see women like that every day. Or like the women in the Almodóvar movie *High Heels*. My God, have you ever seen *High Heels*?

DIANE: That's the only one of his I've missed!

LAURA: Oh, Mom. You have to see it. It's a hilarious melodrama about a mother and daughter.

DIANE: Directors like that help people see the big picture. Without these artists we lose the hidden sides of ourselves. Life in those movies is so much more real than what you see in reality TV.

LAURA: Movies are more real than reality when they're by authentic, beautiful filmmakers, whether it's Hal Ashby or Scorsese or Cassavetes. And by honest actors. That's why actors don't usually like to see stage direction in a script: "sits quietly weeping."

DIANE: How do you know I'm going to be quiet when I'm weeping?

LAURA: Exactly. Even I probably don't know until I'm in the scene!

DIANE: As actors, we can make a new reality onstage. You know, when I was in my thirties doing *A Texas Trilogy* on Broadway, I played three different roles in one night. And one time I gave a lecture to about five hundred women at the Kennedy Center, and this one woman stood up and said, "Ms. Ladd, I have a bone to pick with you! I love your acting, oh yes! But I'm going on fifty. In the third act of *A Texas Trilogy*, you play a woman my age, and I think you wear far too much makeup. You make yourself too old." I replied, "Really?" She nodded, and I continued. "Well, in the first act I play seventeen. Do you feel I wear too much makeup then?" She said, "No, not at all." I said, "Well, in the first act, when I'm seventeen, I don't wear any makeup. I just remember what it's like to be seventeen and I become seventeen. Now, in the second act, I'm a sexy thirty-six, so I wear a lot of makeup. Then comes the third act, your age, and guess what, ma'am? I don't wear any makeup. I just remember my pain in life. And pain makes all of us feel and look older."

LAURA: Wow.

DIANE: It's so funny to me—because we're actresses we're always exploring what's hidden about characters. Do you feel there are things you've had to hide from me about yourself?

LAURA: Hmmm. Well, maybe because you'd been through so much before I was born, I never wanted you to have to worry about me.

DIANE: Why, honey, a mama never stops worrying about her baby. But what you're saying is probably the same with parents. We don't want to burden our children with our fear or need for companionship, so we probably hide that too much. Maybe that's why this is such a vulnerable time. I've never wanted to talk to you about my health. You have enough going on, enough of your own problems to solve.

LAURA: Mom, it breaks my heart that you ever kept how you were feeling from me.

DIANE: Well, we don't know these things until we know. I keep telling my friends: don't wait for the emergency! Don't wait until your loved one is on the other side and you can't reach them. I think everyone should try to ask the questions now and try to accept the answers gently.

LAURA: You are doing great, Mom. How about one more block?

DIANE: When it comes to walking, I am *not* doing great. I'm cold. No more blocks. I'm done.

Laura

Hearing about my mom having to stand up to her parents to pursue her dreams is making me think about how much my mother taught to me to consider my own needs and to push back against authority when it's in opposition to your values. Mom taught me to respect people in charge—to a point. If an authority figure made you feel small in any way, all bets were off.

In my childhood, I witnessed my mom interacting with people with whom she disagreed, and she usually stayed calm. Faced with an argumentative stranger, she would hold it together. Unfortunately, she would lose her cool with cops and school principals—the worst possible people to lose your composure around.

One time in middle school, I worked really hard on a school paper about *Inherit the Wind*. I was using extremist members of the religious right as a modern-day example of fanaticism.

The teacher, as it turned out, was a member of that group. He gave me a poor grade and implied that if I took a different point of view, I would get a better one. My mother marched into the school unannounced, right into the principal's office. I was mortified because I was in middle school and wanted to fight my own battles. But she was rightfully outraged that the teacher thought it was OK to try to manipulate my opinion in that way.

Another time, I was happy for her intervention. When I was about seven at Catholic school, I was sent home because in one of my classes I'd said I believed in reincarnation.

I was very proper and very shy, but that did make me mad. It is one of my first memories of being angry. I said, "I don't understand. Why would God waste a soul? Why do you show up and have only one experience?" It just made sense to me that we would keep trying to figure it out and that a soul would be used again and again, for growth.

The nun teaching that class—the same one who, by the way, also told me that I was "stupid at math"—mocked me in front of the whole class and told me I'd committed a sin by believing in past lives, and she sent me home.

My mother went *insane*.

She ran in there, guns blazing: "Don't you *dare* tell my daughter what she has a right to believe and not believe. You call yourself spiritual? You call yourself *Catholic*? Would Jesus say that she doesn't have the right to have her own beliefs? That she would be *condemned*? That's not Christian!"

She went *off*. The nun had to apologize to me. It was pretty fantastic.

"I'm going to be an actress,
and when I get famous,
I'm going to buy you a beautful
home and make everything OK!"

—DIANE

WALK

MARY
&
PRESTON

LAURA: This is such a pretty park. I have a strong memory of being here as a little child and then of being here every day with Ellery and Jaya. Their preschool was a block away. Ben and I would ride them here on bikes to look at the ocean after school.

DIANE: Why did you raise the kids where you were raised?

LAURA: This part of LA really feels like home to me. It's where my childhood memories mostly took place until I was seven. It makes me feel close to Grandma. And Dad lived at the beach my whole childhood. The Santa Monica Pier feels a little broken, a little battered, but holds something really nostalgic and tender, and it's not as gentrified as some other parts of LA. The pier, the beaches, the lifeguard stations—all of them are the same as when I was little. The car wash. The diner. If only we still had the drive-in in Mar Vista and the ice-skating rink, then everything would be intact!

DIANE: That's lovely, Laura. I'd like to take a break.

LAURA: Nope. Not yet. No way. Do just a little more first.

DIANE: But look, there's a perfect bench.

LAURA: No, Mom, come on. We have to *walk*—that's what the doctor said. We're going to get you off that oxygen soon—we'll have you walking a marathon!

DIANE: Uh, not today we won't. You know, I've had an aversion to walking since the day I missed the school bus and had to walk all the way home from St. Mary's—ten miles! And even on the usual days, I had to walk a whole mile after riding the bus for nine. That killed my walking desire for life.

LAURA: Are we going to have to have this argument every single time? The plan is not to sit, Mom. This is a *walk*. That's what we're gonna do. You can sit the whole rest of the day at home if you want to.

DIANE: I'm so tired today. Let's talk about death.

LAURA: Jeez, you really didn't ease into that, did you? No niceties, just straight to death. OK, let's do it. [*Laughs.*]

DIANE: My dream is to build a mausoleum that has niches for at least eight bodies. And I want to have a bell in there with a little opening in case anybody ever gets locked in. They can ring a bell for help.

LAURA: Oh God, Mom. You think someone's going to get stuck in there? And this is the first I'm hearing about a mausoleum. You wouldn't want to just be buried in nature? Cremated, your ashes scattered on the ocean?

DIANE: No way! [*Laughs.*] I like this body. What if I want it back in the Resurrection?

LAURA: I think at that point God would probably give you a lot of options. Can I ask you something hard? Are you afraid of dying?

DIANE: You know, my daddy used to say, "You never thought about being born and that happened. You don't have to think about dying now. That'll happen too, bet your bottom dollar on that!"

LAURA: I know you think about it, though. Since I was in my early twenties, you've given me written copies of your will every time you leave for a trip: "This is where my jewelry is! This is the lawyer's name!" And every time I see it, the will is different.

DIANE: [*Laughs.*] It's a work in progress! I'm a writer!

LAURA: Well, all I know is I'd hope to have a beautiful death like Grandma Mary's. She was in the hospital for a month before she left us. She had so much time to think about her life.

DIANE: Moments before she died, she said, "Your daddy is waiting for me!" I'm sure he was. Even though they'd been divorced for many years by that point, they still loved each other.

LAURA: Losing my grandma—I can't even put the pain into words. When those white doves were released into the air at the funeral, the love and grief I felt was overwhelming. And I've found myself weeks, months, and now years later seeing something and thinking, *I've got to call Grandma to tell her* . . . and then realizing that I can't.

DIANE: I do that too. I want to call her all the time. And I swear I can hear her voice sometimes. It hurts so much being without her, but that's part of being alive. Our hearts are at risk from the moment we come out of the womb. Life is a great opportunity. And we need to show gratitude. But life is risk. Loving someone is a risk.

LAURA: Yes, so true. I'm trying to be strong but I realize I often don't say what I feel because I'm afraid it will hurt you and this is about you and your health but I have to admit I'm really feeling scared about losing you, Mom.

DIANE: Oh honey, baby, mine. [*Coughs.*] Well, I'm not there yet! One of the doctors said he'd give his whole body to have a heart like mine, strong enough to pull a train! My daddy said something that stuck with me always: "Diane, don't ever forget, by God, you can do anything you put your mind to as long as it's not going to really hurt somebody else or really hurt you. And when you do that thing, you don't ever give up." He repeated that to me again and again: "You don't *ever* give up."

LAURA: And so you've told me many times. I think I know where this story is heading. But go ahead. I'm just happy you're not asking to sit down right now.

DIANE: Do you know the first time he said it to me?

LAURA: Yes, but I think you want to tell me again. Let's walk to that rose garden bench now while you tell me.

DIANE: When I was about five years old, after the war, spinal meningitis was going around where we lived in Chickasaw, Alabama, eight miles from Mobile. And the couple across the road had one son, seventeen years old, and he got spinal meningitis. They took him to the Mobile Infirmary, with beds in the hall—people dying. The doctors actually said to this couple, "Take your son home. I'm sorry, he'll be dead by morning. There's nothing we can do for him." But they couldn't accept that it was all over. They took the son home, and the lady came and pounded on my daddy's door and said, "Mr. Ladner!" She was sobbing. "You've got to come help my son! They say there's no hope for him, but you've got to do something! You're a doctor!" And my father said, "Ma'am, I work with animals—chickens, dogs, cows, and pigs—not people." She said, "I don't care. You're our only hope, the only person nearby who could help my baby. Please come help me." And hearing this, my mama started crying. And finally Daddy said, "All right, you go home. I'll go find a doctor for your son tonight."

LAURA: Wow.

DIANE: She left. My daddy stood in that doorway for a minute. Then he turned and he saw me watching. When Daddy got emotional, his chin quivered so he wouldn't cry. He was a good-looking man. And he stood there, strong and handsome, his chin quivering, and he said, "Diane, you don't ever give up *on* life, as long as you are *in* life."

He walked out that door and searched the county until he found a young doctor who happened to be visiting Chickasaw. He'd just graduated from Johns Hopkins University. My father brought that young doctor to those people's home across the street. I heard the most horrible screaming all night long. But that young doctor worked on that boy, kept working his body so it didn't seize up, getting other people to help him manipulate the boy's spine. And that boy lived. And from then on I knew my daddy was right: you don't ever give up *on* life as long as you are *in* life.

LAURA: That's probably why you fought so hard in the hospital.

DIANE: Yes, and when I was there surrounded by people suffering and moaning, I was reminded that life is precious, something to be enjoyed and to be shared. Thank goodness that you and your beautiful children were there with me.

LAURA: Remember how that room transformed into a magical place when Ellery brought in his guitar?

DIANE: Music and laughter count for a lot! That was so good of him. Even the nurses liked to come in there when he was playing for us. They found our room a place of love and light.

LAURA: You were so full of light and love that one day that we had to cut you off!

DIANE: Oh, right, what was that fantastic shot they gave me?

LAURA: It wasn't a shot. It was a morphine drip attached to a button you could push yourself. And you kept clicking away until you were high as a kite. And one day when Ellery walked in, you shouted to him, "Ellery! I'm on dope!"

DIANE: That's right! Woo! I had some things to say about life that day! He listened with wide eyes, and finally he said, "Nurse! Somebody's got to take that button away from my grandmother!"

LAURA: Ha!

DIANE: Yes, and that wasn't even the best part! The best was my vision when I had my death experience and left my body. I can't express to you how great the joy I felt was, Laura. It was better than any Snickers bar, Christmas present, Oscar, or orgasm. Nothing can ever compare to the bliss. It felt as if my soul left my body and traveled way beyond. I was standing at the entrance of a very large tunnel that was filled with extremely bright light and there was two very tall beings standing at the entrance. I said, "I am not going back," but they responded: "There are things you've left unfinished. Your family needs you." And I think maybe these talks with you may even have been part of that unfinished work.

LAURA: I find that so moving, Mom.

DIANE: Phew! Enough heaviness. Let's talk about something light now! What do you say?

LAURA: Yes! Let's talk more about Grandma Mary and what a flirt she was.

DIANE: Yes, she was a cross between Joan Crawford and Marilyn Monroe. Remember her little joke every time some handyman or mailman came by? "Would you like a cup of coffee?" And they'd say, "Oh, yes, please." And then—in a flirtatious way, mind you—she'd say, "Do you like your coffee like you like your women—strong and sweet?" I'd tell her, "Mother! You can't do that! Some man is going to take you seriously, and good luck!" And she'd say, "Oh, don't be silly. They know I'm joking."

LAURA: She couldn't help it! She was a flirt, a real southern belle.

DIANE: She even flirted with your boyfriends. Remember when Ben came and met everyone for the first time and played us a song?

LAURA: Yes, at my request, Ben played this beautiful song of his, "I Shall Not Walk Alone," for Grandma Mary. Then she slid onto the bench beside him and said, "That was nice. I play too, you know. But I play by ear!" And she hit a bunch of random keys.

DIANE: Ben almost fell off the chair laughing! I think he fell in love with Mary in that moment.

LAURA: She really hammed it up when you got her that part in *Hold Me, Thrill Me, Kiss Me*.

DIANE: Oh, that's right! She stole every scene she was in. Playing trailer park folk, we ad-libbed dialogue about doing laundry and her aches and pains and about the other residents.

LAURA: Did I ever tell you the advice she gave me when I was getting married?

DIANE: No, and I'm afraid to hear it. She was a strict Catholic, and I bet it was something about housekeeping. What did she say?

LAURA: She said, "Do you want to know the secret to a good marriage? Never go to bed angry, and be sure to live by the old saying, 'Be a lady in the parlor, a cook in the kitchen, and a whore in bed.'"

DIANE: Oh God, no! That is indeed an old southern saying—how devastating. I can't believe that she told you that. How disgustingly archaic. I mean, what about the

GRANDMA MARY AND DIANE *HOLD ME, THRILL ME, KISS ME*

man? What's he supposed to be doing in each room? Why doesn't he have to worry about his behavior? You only hear about what women are supposed to do.

LAURA: You're right. And it's a problem because I'm not sure about being a "lady." I don't even know what that looks like... I'm not sure how good of a cook I am, and I'll leave the last one alone. [*Both laugh.*]

DIANE: You know, when she was young, Mary was such a strict Catholic that she was engaged for *four years* to a man named Joe Murphy, another Catholic, and in all that time they kept their promise not to have sex before marriage. She was a virgin engaged for years to Joe Murphy, and then my daddy—handsome, sexy veterinarian Preston Paul Ladner—comes along...

LAURA: Uh-huh. You had two passionate parents.

DIANE: You bet. And then after all that waiting with Joe, Ladner seduced her before they wed, and she got pregnant! Seems she felt guilty and ashamed about it, and so she lied about it to me and to everyone else. It only took me seventy years to figure out the truth. Aunt Johni B accidentally told me that one time my mother said,

"Johni B, don't ever marry a man just because he got you pregnant." And Johni B figured it out.

LAURA: That's true? I never knew that.

DIANE: Yeah, she never told me. She lied about it her whole life.

LAURA: Mom, I hear anger in your voice.

DIANE: Yeah, she didn't care about the truth, as long as her little girl thought she was a good Catholic. I wish I'd been able to tell her when she was still alive that I didn't care! I wasn't her God, just her daughter who loved her to bits! Anyway, it explained why I was a big, healthy, eight-pound baby even though I was born "early." I'm sure everybody knew, but I don't think they cared any more than I did! They were just so happy that Preston had found himself such a beautiful, elegant, and wonderful lady for a wife!

LAURA: My impression is that she had such a hard time in her marriage. Mom, I know you adored him, but Papa did cheat on her a bunch, right?

DIANE: Yes. Daddy actually cried later and said, "I never cheated on your mother for sex. It was only about ego. I thought your Mother had more class in her little finger than any woman I ever met in my life. And somehow I never felt I was good enough for your mama. I loved her so much. Other women chased me. Oh Lord, they did chase me, Diane. And there was a moment in time, off alone, one drink too many . . . and I'd think to myself, *Why the hell not?* It made me feel like I was really something special—like hot stuff!"

LAURA: It's so sad, because it really devastated her, his infidelity.

DIANE: They loved each other, but unfortunately, he succumbed more than once, ruining the marriage. Daddy said, "Cheating cost me the most important thing in my life. I loved your mother. I was a damn fool." A lot of men are damn fools.

LAURA: Thank goodness she got to have some fun later on, after her divorce. And she was a flirt right up to the end. Remember what she gave you for your bridal shower when you married Robert?

DIANE: How could I forget!

LAURA: Everyone else was getting you kitchenware and books. Then she gave you that box from Saks Fifth Avenue with a 1960s-style black sheer negligee inside, like something you'd see on Brigitte Bardot or Marilyn Monroe. The bottom hem was made of faux fur and feathers. All the women there oohed and aahed over it and said, "How sexy!" "Just lovely!"

DIANE: Ha! Yes, and I said, "Oh my God, Mary, this is gorgeous. And I just love that fur along the bottom!" And Mary, age eighty, said, "Yeah, it's to keep your neck warm." That was your grandmother, baby girl.

LAURA: Yeah, the best.

Diane

My daddy, Preston, died when Laura was fourteen. I'm glad we're able to talk about him now, because for all his failings as a husband, he was a wonderful father to me. And because I was an only child I had his full attention.

I spent the first few years of my life in Meridian, Mississippi. Meridian means dividing line. Then, at six, we moved to Chickasaw, Alabama. There were two reasons for the move: first, because my mother's sister, Aunt Bertha, lived in Mobile, Alabama, and was dying of cancer so mother wanted to be fairly close, and also because we were now in World War II. Gas was being rationed so my daddy couldn't get enough to do his needed travel as a country veterinarian. So because he was never a lazy man, Daddy took a job as a pipe fitter foreman at the Chickasaw, Alabama, shipyard. In 1946, after the war ended and Aunt Bertha had gone to be with the angels, we moved back to Meridian. That town had a population of sixty thousand, but still you did not pass another human being on the street without nodding and smiling at them. My father would say, "Hell, even dogs sniff each other. How can human beings pass each other and not acknowledge, 'Hello, other human being!'?"

When I was a little girl, he made me think he could change the weather. We would be in the car, and he knew, of course, it was about to rain. He would say, "Want me to bring the rain for all the flowers and trees, honey?" I'd say, "Oh, yes, Daddy, please." I loved the rain. And he'd chant until the skies opened up. And as the storm was lightening up, he'd say, "Diane, maybe we should call the ol' sun to come visit. You want me to make it stop raining?" And I'd be so excited, and Daddy'd say, "OK." He'd say gibberish and then shout, "Stop raining!" And he'd time it so the rain would stop as he finished his chant. He taught me to believe in magic.

When I was a little girl, he'd say to me, "Girl, I will love you until the ocean wears britches to keep its bottom dry." And when Laura was little, I said that in turn to her.

MARY, DIANE, AND PRESTON

He had a gorgeous voice. He loved country music, and I loved opera, and we both loved singing as we drove down the road on his work trips to sell medicine for chickens. He could write a song in two minutes, and he taught me how. I can write a song about anyone the second I meet them.

Our very favorite was an old folk song that had been sung by workingmen building levees on the Mississippi River. It was recorded by Woody Guthrie in the 1940s as "Crawdad Song."

> *You get a line, I'll get a pole, honey*
>
> *You get a line, I'll get a pole, babe*
>
> *You get a line, I'll get a pole*
>
> *We'll go down to the crawdad hole*
>
> *Honey, baby, mine.*

Our families sung it as long as anyone can remember. It was Laura's favorite bedtime lullaby. She and my dad sang it when they went fishing together. And to this day we use the lyric "honey, baby, mine" as a term of affection.

There are so many stories about my daddy that it's hard to know where to start. When I was ten, he gave me a little .410 gun for my birthday, and he taught me how to shoot well. I learned that a gun is a weapon, not a toy, and that I needed to keep it clean. I used to clean it with a coat hanger and a rag. He said, "If you have something in life, you've got to take care of it." Early one morning, he took me and my little gun hunting. I did not like the idea of hunting because I didn't like the idea of killing. But at least he ate what he killed, and he prayed over it, God bless him. So I agreed to go.

My daddy raised the sweetest, most beautiful bird dogs in the country, so men would come from all around to go hunting with him. On one of these trips, he brought me along. These other men didn't particularly want to take a ten-year-old child on a hunting trip, but he said, "Don't worry. She can keep up."

We tracked through the woods a long time. And finally the dogs took us to a place with deer, and they cornered a beautiful buck on top of a hill. This creature looked like a painting with the sun filtering through the trees.

"Don't say a word," my father whispered to me.

The men all raised their guns simultaneously. My daddy was just about to pull the trigger when echoing through the woods came a little voice: "Run, you little son of a bitch! Run!"

The deer looked up in alarm, and he did run, and he got away.

I saved the deer. But of course my daddy never, ever took me hunting again—which, of course, was fine by me.

Many years later, I was having dinner at the home of Deric Washburn, a writer at the Actors Studio in New York. We didn't have much money, any of us, but Deric knew how to cook, and he made us a delicious meal of chicken livers cooked with wine and yogurt over noodles. I told Deric Washburn my hunting story and he said, "Someday I am going to write a screenplay called *The Deer Hunter*." And he did! And he forgot to call me—they gave the part to a young Meryl Streep.

Years after *that*, when I created the role of Belle Dupree on the TV show *Alice* (based on the Scorsese film for which I created the role of Flo), I made my father a character by improvising stories about him. In my first appearance on the show, I sang a song he wrote, "Uncle Bud," which earned him a screen credit and a check.

When he was dying, he made me promise him that I'd sing another of our favorite songs, "I'll Meet You in the Morning" for him at his funeral. I made it through without crying, but it was one of the hardest things I've ever had to do in my life.

I will meet you in the morning by the bright riverside

When all sorrow has drifted away.

Laura

I loved every second with Grandma Mary. Being with her was everything to me. Mary and I had so many fun times together when Mom was away working. And now that we're doing these walks, I keep remembering so many stories about her that I'd forgotten.

One Halloween, my grandmother and my dad were taking care of me together in Santa Monica while my mother was away doing a play. Dad had bought all this candy for Halloween, but they had no trick-or-treaters. He was so bummed, and Grandma Mary could see how disappointed he was. He said, "Well, this is a wash. I guess I'm just going to go turn on the TV and watch a game or something."

She said, "No! Don't give up! I'm sure they'll come."

Soon after, here comes a ring of the doorbell! A cute little kid dressed like a ghost was at the door to get candy. Dad was so excited that he grabbed the bowl and shouted, "Mary, Mary! We got one!"

The kid at the door grabbed a mound of candy. Dad goes, "Whoa! You just take a couple of pieces."

Dad grabbed the kid's hand and looked at it.

"That is a very old-looking hand," he said. He pulled the costume off the child's head.

It was Mary. She'd thrown a sheet over herself and run out the back door and around to the front of the house.

That's how she was, all the time—mischievous, clever, the best playmate.

My favorite thing to do was to play flight attendant. I was *obsessed* with being a flight attendant! We would set up the dining room chairs in rows. I would make Mary sit and then put all my dolls in the other chairs. I would walk up and down the aisle, offering her and the dolls sodas and magazines. I loved trying to figure out how to carry a tray of drinks without spilling.

We didn't have a washer and dryer, so we would hand-wash clothes with a washboard. She'd have me help her, which I loved because she would always make it so playful. On the back porch we'd set up a big tub of water. At some point she'd throw water all over me and I'd get her back. Then we'd reward ourselves for our hard work by watching *The Andy Griffith Show* and *I Love Lucy* on her little black-and-white TV.

I hurt my mother when, doing press as a young actress, I said that my grandmother raised me when my parents were working. I hated hurting her feelings, but I'd wanted my mother to know that leaving me with her mother when she went to work was the greatest gift she could have given me.

Grandma Mary was my heart and soul—the cutest, most fiery, irreverent, sensual, hysterical dynamo you'd ever meet. She was obsessed with both Elvis Presley and Carly Simon, impeccably mannered and yet a fierce humanitarian.

In much of the country, there's an idea of what a traditional white southern woman from her generation might be like, what she might believe. But in so many ways she defied stereotypes. She grew up Catholic, the child of Norwegian immigrants in a tiny, racially diverse suburb outside of Mobile in the nineteen-teens and -twenties. Her spiritual beliefs and her experience growing up in that community gave her a devout sense of the duty to "honor thy neighbor" and to love and respect people equally.

When the Rodney King incident happened and the riots started, this little woman, then about seventy years old, just about five feet tall, and frail, put a folding table into her little Toyota Corolla and went to the supermarket. She bought a ton of food—bread, turkey, cheese—and then she drove to South Central Los Angeles. By herself, she opened that folding table in front of the AME church, and she made hundreds of sandwiches and started handing them out. When she wasn't handing out sandwiches to people, she was sweeping up broken glass.

That moved me so much. People were in need. A community was war torn. She was just there to help. To me, her memory is a constant reminder to cut through the noise and try to meet people's most basic needs. My mother and I consider it an honor to have the blood of a woman like her running through our veins. There is no one who would ever enter my grandmother's home—not a plumber or workman of any kind—without being given a meal, with cookies and tea. Grandma Mary was always shocked if someone acknowledged these acts of kindness. To her, generosity was as natural as breathing. You'd say she was doing something special, and she'd seem surprised. She'd say, "Oh, it's not special. It's just what you do."

OPPOSITE: MARY AND ELLERY,
MARY AND LAURA IN MOBILE, AL,
GRANDMA MARY AND BELOVED CODY

Me holding my great-grandson

DIANE IN *ALICE DOESN'T LIVE HERE ANYMORE*

WALK

THE SAFETY-PIN CROSS

DIANE: I don't want to walk yet. Can't we just take a break?

LAURA: Hey, why do you seem so crabby today?

DIANE: I don't know what you're talking about.

LAURA: Look at your body language!

DIANE: I'm just tired. My body's tired. Too tired.

LAURA: Too tired for what, Mom?

DIANE: Too tired to live long enough to do everything I want to do. I'm better, but I'm not all the way better. I'm afraid for my grandkids. I'm heartbroken thinking that I'm not going to be around to take care of them. Think of all the wonderful things they have to look forward to! I don't want to not be there.

LAURA: Oh, Mom. It's OK. You're OK! And if you'll just keep walking, it's far more likely that you'll see the kids married and the full deal. How about we go to the next bench?

DIANE: There's a bench *right here*. What do you mean go to the next bench?

LAURA: Mom, it's twelve steps to the next one.

DIANE: I want *this* bench.

LAURA: Twelve steps. Hmm. You know what really got you moving the other day? Talking about acting. Let's try that again. Let's get back into the question of why you weren't sure about letting me act. I mean, we know it can be a tough business, but what else?

DIANE: Don't you remember when you got a screen test for the lead in Adrian Lyne's *Foxes*? Then you didn't get the main part and were just offered a tiny role. When I came home, you were crying on the couch.

LAURA: I was not crying. I might have had a tear in one eye. I was more disappointed than hysterical. You always create a better story than me.

DIANE: Well, you were *sad*. My God, you cannot think of the pain that went through me to see my own little girl, fourteen years old, going through—

LAURA: I was eleven.

DIANE: No.

LAURA: Yeah.

DIANE: No, Laura, you were fourteen, but we told him you were seventeen!

LAURA: No, I was eleven and I said I was fourteen for the role of a seventeen-year-old.

DIANE: My God. What was I thinking? And yet how could we have stopped you? You were so young, but you got a screen test! But when you didn't get the lead and cried over it, that broke my heart. I said, "You see, I don't want you going through this—feeling this rejection!" And you said, "Mother, how do I cope with this? I can't drink—I'm too young! I can't eat a ton of junk food—it would make my face break out! What can I do besides cry?" See, you were smart, even when you were suffering. I wanted you to wait to work. I said, "Train for a long time before you go to work, so by the time you're working you'll be disciplined." I told you that you should polish your gift. I taught you the saying: "How do you get wisdom? Well, the *w* in wisdom stands for the *willpower* to do the *work*. If you drop that *w* off *wisdom*, then you *is dumb*!"

LAURA: Mom, you've told me that saying a million times, and I don't want to stop you doing your thing, but I never needed a speech on discipline. I was very driven. I wanted to study. When we went to dinner at Lee Strasberg's house, he told us that they had children's classes on Saturdays in Hollywood at the Lee Strasberg Theatre Institute.

DIANE: Really? OK. You have a great memory, my child!

LAURA: That same year, when I was ten, I did the kids' summer course at Harvard, where we studied film and body work.

DIANE: And you did that course at the Royal Academy of Dramatic Art in London!

LAURA: Well, that was later, at sixteen.

DIANE: Lucky duck! Mother is jealous! Meanwhile, when I was a girl I was out on country roads with my dad, knocking on doors, selling chicken medicine. What were you seeing in your parents that made you want to act? Was it about making money? Was it glamour? Was it our joy and creativity?

LAURA: I didn't see money then. I didn't see any glamour. I wasn't going to premieres. I did go that one time to the Oscars with you when you were nominated for *Alice Doesn't Live Here Anymore*.

DIANE: That's pretty glamorous. What do you remember? You were seven.

LAURA: I was very proud of the dress you bought me, which was yellow with Swiss polka dots. I had my very magnifying eyeglasses on. When we walked the red carpet, what I remember is that it was so *loud*. Fans were screaming. Photographers were shouting for your attention. I was gripping your hand so tightly that my fingernails marked the palm of your hand. Even though it was a big moment for you, your focus was totally on me. You kept asking if I needed to go to the bathroom. When we took our seats, we saw that Ingrid Bergman was just in front of us. I'd seen a bit of *Casablanca* and so I liked meeting her. And of course a decade later her daughter, Isabella, would become one of my best friends. I remember being so proud of you, Mom. You were happy that people enjoyed the movie. So many people were coming up and saying how much they loved your work and your character. But at one point in the night, I remember walking behind a teenage actress—to me she felt forty but she was probably fifteen—and stepping on the edge of her dress. She turned around and said, "Watch it, bitch!" I was mortified. I thought, *I will never be in the way again.* Even decades later, I remembered that feeling. Whenever I was on tour with Ben or on a friend's set, I'd always be terrified of being in someone's way. I never stepped on another dress hem again, I'll tell you that! And then years later, Naomi Watts and I met doing *We Don't Live Here Anymore*. We were each other's dates to an award ceremony where I was reminded of that night with you. My dress had little holes in the embroidery. Naomi and I were walking together arm in arm, laughing, when I felt a tug on my dress. That memory from when I was seven flooded back. I turned around and another woman's high heel had gotten caught in one of the eyelets of my dress. When I looked up, I recognized a woman who'd slept with an old boyfriend of mine when I was with him. She knew it, and I knew it, and Naomi knew it. We all looked at one another. And then the three of us set about politely freeing my dress from her heel. Walking away, I thought, *If I could be nice under those circumstances, why couldn't that teenage actress have been decent to a seven-year-old she'd never even met?*

DIANE: Amen.

LAURA: It's exhausting to be mean. Why do people make that choice?

DIANE: I agree, but I wonder if you'd have been such a gracious lady if the wound was still raw. It's easier to be kind when time has passed.

LAURA: True.

DIANE: You didn't like the award shows much, but you did wind up liking going to sets with me. When you were six, I drug you—

LAURA: You drugged me?

DIANE: I took you by the hand. You went with me. I *dragged* you to the set of *Alice Doesn't Live Here Anymore*.

LAURA: Oh! That was my all-time favorite. Going back to what we were talking about before about how we fell in love with acting—that time with you on that set really helped shape my dream to become an actor. There weren't a lot of kids around on set. But you were a single parent, and it was summer, and I was well-behaved, so I got to go with you sometimes. Marty saw that I was there, patiently interested, day in and day out. He saw me watching intently, never bored. And so when they were doing a crowded diner scene, he said I should be in it. So I got to be in the movie as an extra. I had been an extra in *White Lightning*, which you did with Burt Reynolds, but I don't think that part made it into the final movie.

DIANE: No, I don't think it did.

LAURA: And that movie set had not been anywhere near as fun for me! I was six. Remember when Matt Clark's character menaced yours with a gun I ran and grabbed your leg to protect you, wrecking the shot? Then that same day, an older girl was eating a popsicle—it was a really hot day—and it stuck to her tongue, and she started screaming, and someone went and got hot coffee to pour on her tongue to unstick it.

DIANE: Oh, it's amazing you went back to a set ever again after that!

LAURA: Well, the *Alice* set was much different and much better. And not only did I get to be an extra, but another day, Marty let me watch a scene you did up close. And I can pinpoint that as the exact moment when I truly fell in love with acting. He showed me into a little hall. There was a door cracked open, and he let me kneel down right beside him looking through the crack while you were shooting that bathroom scene with Ellen Burstyn.

DIANE: I didn't even know about that! Wow!

LAURA: And I loved listening to him talking with you about the importance of getting the details right—from why a certain hairstyle feels right for a character to how your character, Flo, would get angry and what she would do about it. When Mel would piss her off, her palms would sweat. And because you needed to hold dishes, you had the habit of wiping your hands on your uniform before you picked up the plates.

DIANE: God, what a memory you've got.

LAURA: Even at the age of seven, I understood that you and Ellen were these phenomenal actors playing off each other. You showed her your safety-pin cross and said, "Sometimes that's what's holding me together." Where did you even find that cross? I remember it was blue.

DIANE: A wonderful waitress had that cross on her. I said, "I love that cross, honey. I'd like for a character I'm playing, named Flo, to wear it in my new movie, *Alice Doesn't Live Here Anymore*, directed by Martin Scorsese. Where did you get it?" She said, "I made it." I said, "Well, could you make me one for the movie?" She said, "Yes, ma'am, but it would cost you a lot of money." I said, "How much?" And she said, "Ten dollars." I paid it, and she made me that cross that I wore.

LAURA: It was a great detail. And I loved how your character talked about how you spent so much money on your daughter's dental work because your daughter had bad teeth. To this day, that is one of my favorite scenes in any movie. There are two scenes in that movie that, to me, are two of the greatest scenes of women on film. One was there in that bathroom.

DIANE: I love hearing all this. What was the other one?

LAURA: The other was when the two of them are sitting out in the sun, and they're talking, and their eyes are closed for part of it. They're talking about getting lonely and being single and surviving, and they're laughing together. At the end of the scene, the camera cuts wide and the two of them are in lounge chairs, stretched out in the sun in their waitress uniforms in the middle of a Tucson parking lot, next to a dumpster. That's such beautiful filmmaking. I think I really fell in love in that moment with the way images can reveal behavior, expose vulnerabilities.

DIANE: Wow.

LAURA: It wasn't just watching you work that intrigued me. It was your whole group of friends and the way they would talk about acting. I loved hanging out at Shelley Winters's duplex.

DIANE: Shelley was the best! Want to hear how she described her life in her memoir?

LAURA: Of course.

DIANE: "A rocky road that leads out of the Brooklyn ghetto to: one New York apartment, two Oscars, three California houses, four hit plays, five Impressionist paintings, six mink coats, ninety-nine films, and a liberated lady with a smog-stricken palm tree."

LAURA: I love it! What I remember is when I was probably between seven and twelve, she lived on Oakhurst Drive, two blocks from us in the Flats of Beverly Hills. When we'd go over to Shelley's apartment, you guys would sit there on the couch sometimes with Gena Rowlands or Maureen Stapleton or Colleen Dewhurst or Joan Shawlee, who I so loved as the bandleader in *Some Like It Hot*. I would lay on my belly on the cream-colored shag rug in front of the fireplace, next to a terracotta clay bust of Marlon Brando. I can still remember the feel of the soft rug and the sound of your voices. I'd be doodling, or coloring, or doing homework, and I became an invisible witness to this group of women sharing stories about what it's like to be a female screenwriter and producer and trying to get things made. Shelley would tell a story about catching her husband cheating, someone else would talk about confronting a jerk in the studio system. These were women talking with each other about craft and art and digging deep. Other girls my age might have thought that the life of an actress was all about glamour, but what I saw was much more interesting.

DIANE: We showed you movies, too!

LAURA: That's right. You and Shelley were showing me Kubrick movies and French films like *Les Diaboliques*. As a result, when I started as an actress, I really wanted to play *characters*. I was chasing directors who were known for the thing that I watched Scorsese do with you and Ellen. You were never worried about a *Vogue* cover. You weren't afraid to appear on film with no makeup, or as a character who was dangerous, or strange, or difficult. *A Place in the Sun* is a perfect example. The movie is about a poor boy whose connection to a poor girl prevents his getting ahead and marrying the society girl, so he plots the poor girl's murder. Which role do you want to play? The poor, murdered girl, of course, who was played by Shelley, not the pretty society one, who was played—beautifully, I should note—by Elizabeth Taylor.

DIANE: Exactly right.

LAURA: The bravery of playing a character who grates on someone's nerves so much that they do the unthinkable! Because the acting in that film is so great, we can understand his rage, his sense of being trapped, but also feel horrified by him. Shelley didn't shy away from the brilliant choice of giving Montgomery Clift's character a reason to do what he did. The movie doesn't work without that. I mean, what are you going to do? Hire a homely actress and he kills her because she's not pretty enough for him, and he goes off with a goddess? No. You hire Shelley, who is incredibly attractive in her own way but also much more complicated. That was the example I looked to when I got the opportunity to play roles like the ones in *Smooth Talk* or *Blue Velvet* early on in my career. Without growing up around you and Shelley, I don't know if I would have understood those characters or known what to do with them or understood the vulnerability and the complication of the world of David Lynch.

DIANE: Wow! [*Chokes up.*] Laura, just now, in that one moment . . . you made me so proud that I am an actress. This is so exciting. You know, one of the reasons I hesitated in encouraging you into this business is because it is horribly rough. I used to think politics was really bad, but I believe that show business makes politics look like a kindergarten class.

LAURA: But the art makes that stuff worthwhile. And those *dames* trying to make it. I remember a male producer once saying to me, "Ugh, your mom and your godmother are *tough*. Those are *tough* women." It didn't sound like a compliment! I was shocked and confused by his hostility. Only later did I realize what he meant. What he meant was you were honest. You told the truth. You were direct. You would defend other people. If any of you saw a young extra being harassed or treated inappropriately, you'd be the first person running across the set shouting, "Hey! Don't treat her like that!" If you saw injustice, you would voice it. You and your friends were part of my inspiration for the character of Amy Jellicoe in *Enlightened*. Viewers think, *Oh no, here she comes!* You know she's going to screw everything up. But that character has good intentions, and ultimately, she would be the person who gets in the street and makes change. When I first pitched the idea for my character to HBO, my line was, "What if Lucille Ball became Norma Rae?"

DIANE: Ha! I love that.

LAURA: She's one of those people someone like that producer would call tough. Hell yeah, women like that are tough! Because they're going to be the one who says, "That's not OK. You can't treat people like that." Acting was a vocation that allowed for this. When I looked at you and your friends, I thought, *Their job, their life's work, is to tell the truth. Shit, I want to sign up for that job—a job where you're paid to find the truth of the thing.* Your job then becomes an opportunity to have a voice in the world. And because I was introverted, I think I enjoyed that even more, having the opportunity to disappear into characters.

DIANE: Whatever part I have in your education I will happily accept. I remember watching you as a girl in *Mask* with Cher, and you did an incredible acting job, but also you were so disciplined. Without my even telling you to, you did the proper research. You went to this place where a lady taught horseback riding to children who were blind or living with other disabilities. She taught you how to ride a horse as if you were blind! I was so proud of you. I was so impressed with how you used every bit of emotion you had to create this performance.

LAURA: Oh, Mom, thanks. That means so much. You've always talked about loving to act, as long as I can remember.

DIANE: I love the work! Everybody says, "I could be an actor!" It's as if they think, "I could be a doctor" or "I could be a lawyer." *Really?* No. You can't be a good teacher unless you've got a gift. Everybody has a different gift. And Laura, how great you found yours.

LAURA: Thanks, Mom. But also, given that I was not your son but your daughter, did you have other concerns for me, specific to being a girl?

DIANE: Laura, do you have to even ask that? Of course. Every magazine you pick up is using sex as a commodity to sell dresses, makeup, perfume. Remember when we did *Wild at Heart* and I painted my face red? When we got to filming, David had me painting my face with the lipstick. I couldn't help but think about magazines telling women, *"If you use this lipstick, men will all come running to your door!"* And I imagined that my character, Marietta, would think, *If I use the lipstick more, then even more men will run to my door!* The industry demands so much from women, Laura. I didn't want you to face that pressure to look a certain way. You're so beautiful, and I couldn't bear to have a casting agent ever tell you that you weren't. And you know they critique the looks of *every* actress. They always have, and they probably always will. I didn't want that for you.

LAURA: But what's great is that you taught me to seek out radical female characters who weren't defined by their looks and who were complicated. I mean, I got a lead role in *Smooth Talk* when I was fifteen and filmed it when I was sixteen. The girl I played was still a wild innocent and coming into awareness of her own sexuality. But she gets scared when she's pursued by an older man, played by Treat Williams.

DIANE: Yes! That's what I'm talking about! It's so much better to be the complicated woman, not the one on a pedestal! I'm so glad you and I have opted out of the cult of perfection. It's a losing game. Why don't we stop teaching one another that we're not good enough unless we have the perfect dress, the perfect car, the perfect house, the perfect mate, the perfect shoe, the perfect spoon, the perfect meal? Why don't we stop doing that to each other? And that's what show business can feel like. If you're a doctor or a lawyer, no one ever says your backside is too big and, by the way, what is your bust size?

LAURA: Are you asking me my bust size?

DIANE: [*Laughs.*] In this business, people ask things like that all the time!

LAURA: You're telling me! One time in my teens, right before I was about to walk into a scene with a camera behind me, a costume designer handed me a big bag and said, "Put that over your shoulder and carry it in the back so it hides your butt!" She made it seem like it would be really horrible if anyone saw that I had a curvy butt. I remember trying to hide my butt after that, even from boyfriends. It took a long time to get over that. The truth is, even at my skinniest, I've had a booty. I will never not have an ass. I finally realized that I would need to either celebrate it or live in shame.

DIANE: As if that's a bad thing to have! How awful of that costume designer.

LAURA: The actual work of acting when I was young was always so incredible. But the business side of it, the publicity machine, could be brutal. When we were doing press together, especially when I was twenty-three and playing these sex-siren characters, remember how some journalists would say really inappropriate things? I felt so lucky that you and David had my back. I remember one journalist asked you, "How does it feel to have a sex object for a daughter?"

DIANE: Yuck.

LAURA: Exactly. Do you remember what you said?

DIANE: No, what?

LAURA: "I don't know who you're referring to, but I'm definitely proud to have such a great actor as a daughter." And then I think you said to Annett Wolf *[Laura's lifelong publicist]*, "Someone needs to wash that reporter's mouth out with soap!"

DIANE: Wait, see that dog walker over there? He's looking at us like we're fighting. We should smile. See, we're not fighting, young man! We're just a loving mother and daughter yelling about show business.

LAURA: Ha, it's true, people are giving us weird looks.

DIANE: Let them. The actor lives between chance and oblivion.

LAURA: Well, all I know is working with you was fun as hell.

DIANE: Honey, all I know is that I was born to be an actress and so were you. [*Coughs.*]

LAURA: Here's the good news, Mom. Either you love a good story, you love talking about the movie business, or you enjoy your daughter talking so much that we've passed three benches.

Laura

A few years ago, I found something that Tennessee Williams had said about my mom to a journalist, and it floored me: "[Diane] is like a splash of Tabasco sauce; tart, tasty, and capable of turning the bland into something exotic. I've been overwhelmed by her candor in both her work and her life.... Her grasp of God—and the manner in which His angels compel the creative artist—is firmer than that of anyone else I've known. From those who have worked with her, I've heard that she has, between her technical outpouring of craft and her mental, emotional creation of acting art, the thinnest layer of gauze. Meaning that she is perfectly clear, as Shakespeare told us all artists should be."

I love what Tennessee said about Mom's talent. It's so true. And not only of how she is as an actor but I also saw that rawness, that transparency, in how she raised me. I don't know that you can separate the two, the mother and the artist. That quality in her is what inspired me the most to act without an agenda, without playing chess, without hiding behind veils, pulled not only in front of others but also in front of oneself. I long for that kind of clarity in art and in life.

You hope every time you're looking in the eyes of another actor that everything else goes away, and suddenly you're telling each other the truth about your lives. And it doesn't matter what the story is that gets you there, it's the vulnerability, the availability, the sharing of something so tender, and so enraging, and so complicated, and so funny, that just makes you one, like you're family, even if you're strangers. But if it's your mother, it's all those things a million times over. There's no one else you have that much of a shared story with—not your husband or wife. You share a chapter with them, but often your parent shares your lifetime, and knows you even before you know yourself.

"Diane is like a splash of Tabasco sauce; tart, tasty, and capable of turning the bland into something exotic."

—TENNESSEE WILLIAMS

WALK

BENT
SPOONS

LAURA: Today, Mom, I wanted to start this walk off by praising you for how far you've come already. Even through this health challenge, I've never seen you as a person who just *survives*. You live with such passion. And we're getting you healthy, aren't we? Now we just need you to take those vitamins we talked about.

DIANE: How many times do I have to tell you? I don't want to take any more damn pills, Laura! It's enough!

LAURA: OK. Jeez. I'll lay off. And I'll go back to complimenting you. You're so determined. I've heard Ben say to the kids, "Nana always has a dream. She never gives up on her dream."

DIANE: That ex-husband of yours—he knows about dreams. And he certainly found his incredible gift. And he's right—I have always had faith. It probably has something to do with how I grew up. You know, because my given first name was Rose, I was enamored with Saint Rose of Lima, Peru. She had long hair like I did. When I was thirteen, I was very impressed by her. She cut off all her hair so she wouldn't be attractive to boys. I decided I wouldn't cut off my hair. If I did, I might decide I didn't want to be a saint and it'd be too late—I'd just be a regular girl nicknamed Baldy.

LAURA: Very practical. You seem to have enjoyed Catholic school.

DIANE: Well, the nuns at St. Mary's Church in Mobile, Alabama, impressed me. To be more like them, I would go over to the church each day, sit in a pew, and I'd stare at the statuettes to see if one of them would come alive and appear to me. I'd give up my lunch hour to that activity. Every day I would go over to pray. And then one day when I was in the fifth grade, the nun came in and said, "Children, which one of you is running over to church at lunchtime?" The other kids thought I was going to get it. They said, "Diane! Diane does it!" The nun says, "OK, Diane. I want to tell you there's a letter here from this man and I'm going to read it to you."

LAURA: Oh, right. This is vaguely familiar. Didn't you save someone's life or something? Weren't you involved in helping save someone's life?

DIANE: Well, this man's wife and child had been killed in an accident. He was on his way to commit suicide, and he saw this little child going to church on her lunch hour. He stopped and he said to himself, "If she's going in there, either there's something awfully bad in her life she's got to ask God to help her with, or she's going in to ask God to help the world." Either way, he said, "If a little child can have that much faith and give up her lunch hour to go in, why can't I keep living and help make the world a better place for other people?" The nun said, "Diane, that man decided not to kill himself because he saw you praying. So you just keep up that good work."

LAURA: Amazing. When I was a kid, I always knew that you and Grandma both had resounding faith. It made me take faith seriously, seeing how much sustenance it brought you. Catholicism is so theatrical. I loved the storytelling of it all, the parables, the idea of angels. And it's not just Catholicism—I even like to believe in flower fairies. Being a believer makes for a more interesting life, don't you think?

DIANE: Yes, it really does. I'm so glad to hear that.

LAURA: You and Grandma definitely gave me that rooted belief in something larger than what we see. That's helped me a lot of times I've felt out of control or afraid. I can have a deep trust that there's something bigger happening. You exposed me to so much spiritually as a kid. And I am so lucky because you really did make me aware of so many paths. Grandma gave me the ritual and tradition of Catholicism. But while I was being given that, you were simultaneously telling me what you didn't agree with. I love that you were never big on the shaming part of organized religion. And I was so lucky that you taught me to be open to my own unique, spiritual path, whatever that would look like. I will never forget that in church on Sundays when we would say the Nicene Creed—particularly the part that goes "I believe in one holy catholic and apostolic Church"—you would lean over and whisper, "You don't have to say that part if you don't want to. You don't have to believe in one path. There are many roads to God." When I was eight, you taught me to meditate. We would go to mother-daughter yoga class and learn breathing techniques. At twelve I was a pro-choice Catholic who believed in reincarnation. I think that's why I later studied Sanskrit at Loyola and gave my daughter a Sanskrit name.

DIANE: Well, I'm honored by that. You know, I was just remembering how when I was growing up, my first boyfriend, when I was six, Joe Pat Caskey, was Catholic, and when I was seven, my boyfriend was Jewish, Louis Rosenbaum.

LAURA: You had two boyfriends before age seven? I didn't have a boyfriend until my junior year in high school!

DIANE: You know, Catholicism influenced me positively in many ways, but it also gave me a bit of a savior complex.

LAURA: You still have something of a savior complex, Mom! I love how many stories there are of you saving someone's life in one way or another. I know they're all true, but it's almost unbelievable.

DIANE: It *is* all true. And you're one to talk. Didn't you want to be a saint too when you were growing up?

LAURA: Of course. I wanted to be Saint Bernadette, the patron saint of the ill and the poor.

DIANE: One of my all-time favorite songs is "Song of Bernadette"! It's about filling your heart with courage, understanding, and wisdom. Saint Bernadette was a poor fourteen-year-old girl when the Virgin Mary appeared to her at Lourdes in 1858. She held fast to what she believed even as the rest of the world tried to sway her.

LAURA: Yes, and as a little girl, I imagined I was her. When I was six, I used to dig in the backyard with teaspoons. I assumed that if I was a saint like Bernadette, holy water was going to gush forth, and I could heal everybody in the neighborhood. Grandma Mary kept finding spoons bent and twisted by the tire swing. She'd ask me, "What have you been doing with all my spoons?"

DIANE: Precious. That's better than what I did in our backyard as a little girl. My grandma found me out in the yard and said, "Why are you eating dirt?" I said, "Somebody told me it's good for me and would keep me healthy." And my grandmother said, "Let that child eat dirt if she wants to."

LAURA: Well, that was lucky for you. I got a spanking from Grandma Mary!

DIANE: No!

LAURA: Yes! Because I ruined her yard and bent all her spoons. She got so mad at me. I was so mad about the spoons too! I'd been feeling so spiritual and connected to God. I was praying so hard. I was so holy. By day five of digging, I was flinging the spoons around, shouting, "Damn! Bernadette, where's the frigging holy water, and why the hell aren't you appearing to me?" Which reminds me: Grandma also washed my mouth out with soap.

DIANE: Oh no, why? Did you talk back?

LAURA: No, never! It was for cursing. Bellina and I did cuss like sailors. We used to tape-record ourselves saying every dirty word we could think of as fast as possible, in the voice of Howard Cosell. And then a boy at school taught Bellina and me a rap. Let's just say it began, "I hate to talk about your mom but she's in my class. She's got popcorn titties and a rubber ass—" At which point I was lifted by the seat of my Catholic schoolgirl uniform, and the next thing I knew, I had a bar of soap in my mouth.

DIANE: Yes, but you never cussed again.

LAURA: Are you fucking kidding me? Maybe it's why I cuss so *much*.

DIANE: Well, Mary never should have spanked you for the bent spoons. She should have given you a hug and been proud of you. That kind of faith and belief can make somebody a great actress or a great doctor, a great anything. I'm sure if the holy ones did ever look down and see that holy a child, they'd have smiled on you. I bet you put one heck of a smile on Bernadette.

LAURA: At least she could have magically helped me unbend the spoons!

DIANE: Ha! I made sure to give you some amazing godparents so you'd have a good spiritual education. Shelley had that tree in front of her apartment, and every time she went anywhere—

LAURA: She would stop and put both hands on the tree and bless it!

DIANE: That's right! And she would say, "God made a tree." And speaking of Shelley and trees, one time, Shelley threw a big Christmas party and invited a lot of people from her temple. I was over in one corner, and a lady from her temple came over to me and said, "Shelley Winters has a *Christmas tree*!" She said it with an edge.

And I said, "Yeah."

"Why does Shelley have a *Christmas* tree?"

And I said, "I don't know. Why don't you go ask Shelley?"

She said, "I will." She walked over to Shelley and said, "Shelley, you have a Christmas tree!" Shelley replied, "Yes, isn't it wonderful! I never had a Christmas tree as a child, and I always wanted a tree, and now I have one!"

The woman said, "But Shelley, a tree is *Christian*. A tree represents *Jesus*."

And Shelley in a tight, stern voice, pointing her finger at the woman, said, "Don't you say anything about that man! Jesus was Jewish and so am I! And don't be reductive! He had a lot more going for him than *Christmas trees*! Just look at the following he's got today!"

LAURA: She was the best.

DIANE: Oh my God, I just remembered a New Year's Eve party I went to with her at the writer Norman Mailer's house. We entered the foyer on time, and Norman wasn't even downstairs yet. We were told he was still getting dressed. There was nobody else around except a caterer organizing appetizers.

"The place is shockingly unkempt," Shelley said to me. "Look how dusty these staircase banisters are!" And they really were.

We didn't have anything else to do while we waited, so we cleaned off the banisters.

A few minutes later, Norman made his grand entrance, took one look at the banisters, and said, "Where's my cocaine?"

I think we must've wiped away about a million dollars' worth!

LAURA: Oops! That's hysterical. You know I always think about how she loved Johnny Carson but she was often the butt of his jokes. That can't have been fun. Was she hurt by that?

DIANE: You think she would have been but she had so much fun with him and loved being on Johnny's show. Did you ever see a clip of her on Johnny Carson with Oliver Reed, who played Bill Sikes in *Oliver!*?

LAURA: No! I remember we visited her one time on set when she was making a movie with him.

DIANE: Well, in 1975 they were on *The Tonight Show* with Johnny Carson together and Reed was horrific. He kept talking about how women are happy in the kitchen and how women's lib was a bad idea. He said, "A woman's place is looking after her man and her children." And he kept shushing her and women in the audience. Shelley was offstage at the time, but she came back on and dumped a glass of water on his head!

LAURA: Oh my God, what a badass!

DIANE: You know, Shelley often played the dumb blonde, but she was brilliant and sometimes out of nowhere would push back in a radical way. Her ability to ride that line is part of why she was so popular on late-night TV.

LAURA: Yes, that's why Johnny loved her. When I think of her, I think of such a strong, outspoken woman. Man, I hate that she ever felt she had to play the game. I'm so grateful you made her my godmother. Thank you.

DIANE: You're welcome. And on that note, let's head back to the car. I think this was plenty for today.

LAURA: Come on, Mom, let's do a little more.

DIANE: I've got to stop. I'm tired, honey. I really am.

LAURA: But Mom, it's just a—

DIANE: No! I said I'm tired.

LAURA: Mom, we have to. The doctor said—

DIANE: Will you fucking stop it, goddamn it? This is my body! And you don't have to kill me trying to save my life. No more pushing. I mean it. I said it's *enough*.

LAURA: OK, OK. I'm sorry. I'll get the car. (over the shoulder) I guess you still cuss too?

Laura

It's difficult to know how hard to push Mom. On one hand, I want to make her exercise more than she thinks she can. On the other hand, I know she's frail and I don't want to upset her. When should I be her cheerleader? When should I be her nurse? When should I push her for stories? When should I give her space?

A year ago, I would have waited for her to say whatever she wanted in her own time. I want her to know that if she's scared of dying, she's not alone. But at the same time, I don't want to cause her any more grief by sharing with her how upset I am.

And yet, who told us that we're supposed to be nothing but upbeat around people who are sick and dying? Why is it that we are supposed to go into their hospital rooms saying, "You look great! You're hungry today? That's a good sign! You'll be out of here in no time!"?

What if these walks are my last chance to hear her stories? I can't pass up this opportunity to tell the truth: "You look tired. We don't know how much time we have left. There are so many things I want to ask you before it's too late."

GREEN LEOTARDS
& SHOW FOLK

DIANE: Laura! This morning I talked to the Environmental Working Group and to the agricultural commissioner. We've got to get members of the community who've also been dealing with this pesticide that's hurt me. We need to write to the governor. We have to stop the use of glyphosates.

LAURA: Mom, you are incredible. I was actually going to tell you that I did what you asked and talked to your neighbor and to the environmental attorney. We are all on top of this. But I have to say, you're such a badass! Here I'm worried about you having enough energy to walk a few steps, and you've already spent three hours on calls today talking about petrochemicals. And not to protect yourself, but to protect others from what hurt you. You blow my mind.

DIANE: So, Laura, what are we going to talk about today?

LAURA: Let's talk about your environmental activism!

DIANE: No, after having been on these calls for hours, let's please talk about something else!

LAURA: OK, how about this: thinking about your activism, I just had a flashback to that Equal Rights Amendment rally you and Jane Fonda and Ed Asner took me and Bellina to when we were eleven.

DIANE: Oh, right! You two were so cute in your green leotards.

LAURA: Yes, that morning we woke up all excited to march, and you said the color of the event was green, so we put those on. And then do you not remember what you did to us?

DIANE: What did I do?

LAURA: You were giving a speech up in front of thousands of people in this park in downtown LA and you said: "My daddy taught me a song! This song meant everything to me. And now I'd like to introduce you to my two backup singers!" And Bellina and I looked at each other in horror as we realized that you meant us. You dragged us onstage and made us sing in front of thousands of people with no warning. The horror of being eleven and having to perform in green leotards! It was basically child abuse. But you were like, "C'mon, girls! We're show folk! This is what we do!"

DIANE: Well, we are. And even though the ERA didn't pass, that work was important.

DIANE, 16

Santa Monica Pier, age 2

LAURA

high school graduation

Crystal Scarborough, swimming lessons

first communion

age 6-7

age 6

age 9

age 8

Aunt Averil and Diane

Bellina and Laura

To Mom
Love Laura D.

LAURA: You must have had such a hard time when you were starting out. When I see photos of you at the age of sixteen, I think you were *so young* to be in New York City with no money, knowing no one, with only a dream to become an actress!

DIANE: I knew what I wanted to do.

LAURA: But you must have been so vulnerable! If a guy was going to mess with me on a set, they were crazy because people knew my parents. Dad was the guy who shot and killed John Wayne in *The Cowboys*. I figure Dad's tough-guy persona saved me from some real shit. Not that guys were never inappropriate, but in terms of really being in danger, I feel like my family's reputation offered me a little protection that other actresses my age didn't have. And like them, you had no one! And that era was so different! I mean, as a teenager, you had to wear heels to every audition, right?

DIANE: Oh my, yes. On an interview, you didn't wear slacks, and you had to dress to the nines. When I first started out as an actress, I had a manager who said, "Make sure there's no rip in your stocking!" That manager didn't worry about his male clients having a rip in their socks. And your heels could not be scuffed. Your clothes had to be pressed. You needed your hair done and makeup flawless. And you had to make sure that damn seam up the back of your calf was straight.

LAURA: I'm glad you eventually rejected that hyperfeminine thing so many of our relatives in the South had. Grandma Mary always had her hair set if she left the house. She would never go to the market without lipstick, ever.

DIANE: Reese used to put her hair in curlers, right?

LAURA: Totally. All you southern girls were raised with the credo of "putting your face on." I first heard the expression when Mary Kay Place said it in *Citizen Ruth*. It reminds me of one time when Reese and I were doing press. We'd done a few interviews, and our makeup and hair team had left. On a quick break, she said, "Dern, look through your purse. Gimme some lipstick." I pulled out a lipstick and I handed it to her. She looked at me as if I'd handed her a Sharpie and said, "Dern, that's not lipstick. That's *brown*."

DIANE: Ha! Of course, as a southern lady, she thinks of lipstick as always either pink or red.

LAURA: Reese is able to get out of it when she's working, and be totally raw, as she was in *Wild*. And I think she and I would agree that a lot of that way of being a vulnerable woman on-screen started with you and the other great rebel actors we worship from seventies cinema. I can't remember you having full makeup on for anything but work. Makeup aside, though, you're still a Mississippi kid who found her way into this world. You've never let anyone wait on you, and you've always been a hard worker. I mean, you love a bedazzled baseball cap, but you never went in for posturing.

DIANE: True. And, well, that's lovely of you, but there are so many others who had to fight even harder to get out from under the pressure to be glamorous! How about Jane Fonda? She had a movie-star father! And she appeared in *Barbarella*, but she wanted to be a serious actor. So she fought for it, and she did *Klute*, and *Coming Home* with your father. Laura, she produced that herself! My God, such hard, emotionally raw stories she's given us.

LAURA: Remember when Shelley took me to the Grauman's Chinese Theatre 1978 premiere of *Superman*?

DIANE: Yes, I was out of town working somewhere.

LAURA: She wore no makeup, a white T-shirt, false eyelashes, a full-length fur coat, and sneakers. It's such a good look—although you and I would wear fake fur. She was walking down the red carpet, and I was holding her hand, and people were shouting, "Shelley! Shelley! Why are you seeing *Superman*?" and she said, "I'll see anything with Marlon in it." Marlon Brando was playing Jor-El. I was twelve and couldn't get over the length of her false eyelashes.

DIANE: She wore those always! She said they made her eyes sparkle.

LAURA: That was very you at that time too—no makeup, a light lipstick, and always those big false eyelashes, even if you were just at home with her having a scotch and soda.

DIANE: Shelley never drank, not really.

LAURA: Yeah, but it was just the women being together, you might put on false eyelashes just to feel good together. I loved that so much. So unceremonious, with such an un-Hollywood lack of affect, lack of need for the biggest house, lack of a desire to put your face on before people come over. I wanted to play characters who weren't trying to be what they weren't, who could be out there with untamed hair, in sweatpants and a T-shirt. For me as a little girl, what I witnessed were these women who let themselves be known in all their complexity. I saw their pores. Their skin was never covered up with tons of makeup. It was something really profound to me about who I wanted to be if I was going to be an artist—the kind of woman who carries herself with deep authenticity in her life, in her style, in the way she lives, in the way she shares stories with her friends, in the way she's willing to be vulnerable. You were complicated and direct, and that's how I will always try to be because of your example.

DIANE: What beautiful memories, and what a great testimonial. I lived it and don't see it as clear as you!

LAURA: On the subject of glamour, one thing I've always wanted to ask you about is when you were still young and you had to really doll yourself up, like when you worked at the Copacabana. Was that just awful?

DIANE: Being a Copa girl was actually *so* much fun, Laura.

LAURA: You were never harassed there?

DIANE: Oh my, no. You would do the show, and then you would sit at a table and look beautiful as part of the ambiance. We were expected to be very professional, and to look as elegant as possible in our expensive costumes. However, we were never required to mingle with any guests. In fact, it was quite the opposite! You could look at us, but not touch! No one dared approach our table without permission. The only time a man would approach us was if someone was taking a publicity picture or a celebrity was allowed to come over and compliment us on the show. If anyone else came toward our table, immediately several men in tuxedos who looked an awful lot like mobsters would come out of the woodwork and say, with deadly looks, "Where are you going, sir?" My group included twins who were not only great dancers but also waterskiing champions, a magazine cover model, and a young actress who'd just graduated from London's RADA and later married the actor William Shatner.

LAURA: Weren't you ever preyed upon?

DIANE: Of course, like any woman, I did have those experiences. Some were in childhood. Once I was walking home alone from school, and a man in a white car came really close by the curb and said, "Hi, little girl, would you like some candy?" Having been trained by my mother, I said, "I don't want any candy!" and I ran up to the nearest house and pretended to live there. From the steps, I yelled, "I'm going to tell my mother you just tried to get me in that car and give me some candy!" And he took off.

LAURA: How old were you?

DIANE: Seven.

LAURA: Oof! You know what's sad? I hardly know anyone who wasn't assaulted or harassed at some point in their childhood.

DIANE: You're bringing back so many memories. When I was seventeen and trying to break into film, I got invited to go to my first movie set. I borrowed my girlfriend's suit, stuffed my bra, and put on heels. On the way, I was getting honked at and stopping traffic, so I must have looked pretty good.

LAURA: I believe it. Here's a photo of you I just found online that I'd never seen. Do you remember this?

DIANE: Oh my God. Look at that. That's a still from *The Steagle*. 1971. The director wanted me to act like Marilyn Monroe. That is a very Marilyn dress. He also wanted me to play my character with crossed eyes the whole time, but I said I couldn't do it because I refused to ruin my eyes. But my God. Look at that bust! I must've had stockings and a bunch of other stuff tucked into the sides to push that up! But those are my real legs! Lookin' good, DL!

LAURA: But go back to the story.

DIANE: Right. My friend introduced me to Spencer Tracy. As he and I shook hands, a crew member made a dirty "jerk-off" gesture behind my back.

LAURA: Ew!

DIANE: Exactly. I didn't see it, but I saw Spencer's appalled reaction, and someone told me what had happened. Spencer, who was a gentleman, said, "We're going to sit you here next to the camera so you can see everything that's going on." Where, by the way, I would be out of the crewman's reach. Spencer was polite, gracious, and loving. He had cancer, so he stopped at five thirty every day. When five thirty came that day, they were in the middle of a scene, so the director, Stanley Kramer, asked him if he could please push through and finish the scene. He agreed but asked the same crew member who'd made the lewd gesture for a glass of water, because his throat was hurting. The guy said, "Get it yourself. I'm not your slave." Spencer said, "What did you say?" "I'm not your slave."

LAURA: What a revolting comment. And, my god, to be so disrespectful to Spencer Tracy too.

DIANE: Spencer walked over and said, "No, but you're a parasite. You've been sipping beer, playing poker. You disrespected a young lady; you're a rude man and you're a mean man. I saw you last night shoving some extras. You're a disgrace to your fellow crewmen and you're a loser. You're being paid and you're doing nothing. I'm going to finish the scene, and if there's no glass of water when I get back, from now on I'll

Copyright ©1971, Avco Embassy
Pictures Corp. All rights reserved.
Permission granted for News-
paper and Magazine reproduction.
Made in U.S.A.

IN COLOR

Joseph E. Levine presents
An Avco Embassy Film
THE STEAGLE
An Avco Embassy Release

Property of National Screen Service Corpora-
tion. Licensed for use only in connection with
the exhibition of this picture at the theatre
licensing this material. License signed not to
trade, sell or give it away, or permit others
to use it, nor shall licensee be entitled to any
credit upon return of this material. This material either must be returned or destroyed
immediately after use.

71/146

RICHARD BENJAMIN AND DIANE IN *THE STEAGLE*

ban you from this set, even if I have to pay your salary while you stay at home and sit on your backside." At the end of this scene, the water was there. The other crew guys loved Spencer Tracy.

LAURA: Wow. What a guy. Also, Mom, didn't you tell me some casting-couch story once?

DIANE: Which one? I mean, I was so innocent I would walk through evil and not even know. One time a coworker's brother said he'd drive me home. I was broke—the other chorus girls and I would go to a bar and order a beer and then eat all the bread and butter we could stand because we couldn't afford proper meals. So I was happy for a free ride home. He said he just had to pick something up at his motel. He invited me in and said, "Make yourself comfortable," and then he attacked me. I fought him off, but that was scary. I can tell you that Hollywood has some bad people. I guess everywhere does.

LAURA: But what was the other story you have, about the poolside meeting?

DIANE: Oh, that. Oh, baby, you just want to keep me talking so I keep walking! I got your number! [*Laughs.*] Anyway, I was spotted in a dance show and invited for lunch and a swim by the famous president of Columbia Pictures, Harry Cohn, who was then about sixty. He said he thought I showed promise and had "a youthful look." I did—because I was sixteen! I put on a black velvet bathing suit and showed up for the meeting. He told me to sit next to him, and I did. He asked me what I wanted to drink. When I asked for lemonade, he laughed. He and his henchmen were drinking cocktails. But I was brought a lemonade. As I was drinking it, he took his hand and slapped it down onto my thigh, right next to my crotch. I froze and looked at him, shocked. Then I picked up his hand and threw it back at him. As I got up to leave, he said, "You'll never be a star that way, honey."

LAURA: You showed him.

DIANE: Uh-huh. Am I a star yet? I just slept with people I fell in love with, or who I married! [*Laughs.*] I like to think I protected you from all that, but I worry that you still saw some of it.

LAURA: Well, of course. When I was thirteen, I'd do auditions with fifty-year-old directors alone in a hotel room at the Chateau Marmont. Why wasn't the casting director in the room? Why did it have to be like that? Why was I asked to sit on a bed to read? A number of times, I was alone in a room with a director, sitting on a bed to read, which never felt comfortable or safe. By good fortune, those were not moments where men took advantage. It's nothing a young actor or actress should ever deal with, and luckily, they would most likely not have to deal with that now.

DIANE: Chilling. Did anything really bad ever happen to you on those auditions?

LAURA: Like you, Mom, I have been around dangerous people. Fortunately, if something got creepy, there was always someone there to rescue me at the last minute. You know what's so tragic, and disturbing for so many women—and young girls and boys—is that often when it feels inappropriate and scary is when you shut down. Luckily for me, I don't have a story of severe trauma to share with you, but I definitely was often uncomfortable and knew that something wasn't the way it should go, but I didn't bring it to you. I thought I should trust the adults and not complain. That's bullshit, of course. That's an old model that I pray your grandkids' generation has wiped away. Your teacher, your priest, your coach—or your director or costar—may be the last person you should trust. That's a heartbreaking truth that I think young people know now.

DIANE: And it's not always men doing that kind of thing. Roger Corman, who gave so many people I know big breaks—me, your dad, Jonathan Demme, Jack Nicholson, Harry Dean Stanton, Susan Strasberg, Peter Bogdanovich, and on and on—told me that one girl trying to get a job offered herself to him and literally chased him around his desk while he ran for his life.

LAURA: I think that was probably a much rarer situation than your poolside meeting. But I think it's important to acknowledge that women can be awful too. It goes back to middle school. A girl would say, "Oh my God, I was in the bathroom. And so-and-so said that you're sooo not her best friend anymore. Just so you know." I think we've been doing that since seventh grade. I don't think boys are sitting around in middle school talking about how they're better friends than the other boys. And especially in your era, if a woman got the one seat at the table designated for women, the boys were looking at her like, "Well, you better show us you're not going to make girly decisions here."

DIANE: And then they'd be as sexist as any man!

LAURA: I worked with a couple of women in and around film and television who were made to feel that they needed violence or nudity, and they would push people in one direction or the other without considering how a young woman might feel about certain choices. I mean, it wasn't until the last few years that even you and I started talking more deeply about all this! You know what I was thinking about the other day? That horrible crew member on that set who was always manhandling us.

DIANE: Oh! He was the worst!

LAURA: Why did we take so long to say anything about him?

DIANE: Well, we did eventually, after he lifted my skirt up in front of everyone.

LAURA: That's right. Finally we said enough is enough. We had to stop just commiserating with each other and bring it up to the people in charge. Yeah, but even then, instead of anyone implying that they were sorry we had this experience, they were worried about making him feel bad. That was the whole focus: how to help him understand why his behavior needed to change. But they wanted to make sure he knew that he could keep his job. And we were part of that too: "Maybe if there's any way you could just be more mindful because it made us feel uncomfortable..." Why were we so nice about it? He was deeply impacting our ability to do our job! It was not good for anybody, and yet we were uncomfortable making him feel embarrassed or bad and in no way, shape, or form had it crossed our minds that we would ever want to see him *fired*.

DIANE: Well, I understand our reluctance. Every crew member on most sets is male. If there's a nude scene or delicacy required and you need help with something, it feels like there's no one else there to help you. You don't want to make the people responsible for lighting you and feeding you and dressing you mad.

LAURA: So many bullies fall because one person is brave enough to come forward. Then so many others know that their experience wasn't an isolated incident. And I have to point out that we are two privileged white actresses. We've dealt with all this bad behavior, but the women of color we know have had it so much worse when it comes to the lack of roles, consideration, and opportunity. My God, at least we're seeing some shifts now in not only casting but crew and production. In safety on set, thank God, but also in terms of gender and diversity parity. Luckily, there are more and more companies and producers ensuring that any work environment we enter reflects the way the real world looks.

DIANE: It's about time! And if you think what it was like when you started out was bad, can you imagine when *I* started? On sets there were no women on the crew and not one person of color. In the theater it was different. I certainly worked with much more diverse casts and crews in theater than in TV and movies. Things are better now in that regard, but, man, it's taking a long time . . .

LAURA: Even when I started, twenty years after you, on my first movie there were no women on the crew. Men did my makeup and hair.

DIANE: Sadly, I'm not surprised.

LAURA: I look at Jaya and Ellery's generation, and they are so much more aware and so much more comfortable in their own skin. They're growing up in a different world than we did. Filling out paperwork at a doctor's office the other day, Jaya said, "Wait, what are these questions? Race, religion? They have no right to ask me these questions!" It would never have occurred to you or me that we didn't answer the questions we were asked! Jaya's mantra is, "Nobody's going to tell me to shut up!" I'm so inspired by her confidence.

DIANE: Me too.

LAURA: Speaking of which, I should get back to her now. Let me get you home. You did great today! No coughing, huh?

DIANE: Well, I'm exhausted. I'm going to sleep for a week.

LAURA: Not a week. Remember, we're doing this every day. See you first thing in the morning.

Laura

Talking with my mom about the pressure to look good and to navigate uncomfortable situations has taken me right back to middle school. I'm realizing that my mom helped me avoid so much of that need to fit in that young girls often have—understandably, because we've been raised on images of perfection and taught to chase archetypes of what it means to be pretty or perfect.

In our household, imperfection was both the family business and the favorite pastime. Mom and I weren't getting manicures together. We were watching Hal Ashby movies. (Actually, I wouldn't have minded a mani-pedi now and then.) Still, there were times when I felt the pull of social pressure and had to look to my mom for help navigating it.

At my middle school we had to wear uniforms, but the rich girls still found a way to compete. We were only in eighth grade, but they would come in with Louis Vuitton purses.

When I told my mom about this, she could have said, "Let's get you a purse!" Instead she listened, and then she said, "Laura, what makes you feel good about yourself? What kind of clothes do you like?"

I said, "I like bright colors."

"OK," she said. "Well, I know you have your uniform, so you're limited there, but what bright accessory do you want to wear?"

I said, "We can wear whatever socks we want, and I always thought it'd be so cool to wear knee-high socks in bright colors."

Her eyes lit up. "Oh my God, you've got to do it!" she said.

She made me feel clever, and like we were about to embark on a big adventure revolutionizing my wardrobe together. She bought me a bunch of wild knee-high socks.

The next day, I put on my gray-and-white uniform like usual, but instead of the typical little tennis-ball athletic socks and Capezios like all the other girls wore, I pulled on a pair of bright-red, almost Day-Glo socks and my saddle shoes.

"What are you wearing?" one of the girls said, her voice dripping with disapproval.

"Aren't they *great*?" I said.

All day, I was mocked, but I thought I looked good, and that was all that mattered. So I think that was a revelation: that "perfection" for me meant finding my own thing, not playing the game everyone else was playing. My mom helped me find a new game.

Every day after that, I showed up to school in crazy socks. The other girls got bored of teasing me because I would just roll my eyes when they did. And guess what? No matter what you do, some people are going to be mean, and some people are going to love you, and that's what life is.

And then, when I started acting around that same time, the roles I took were not about looking hot or like everyone else.

Case in point: *Ladies and Gentlemen, the Fabulous Stains. Stains* is a 1982 cult movie directed by Lou Adler and written by Nancy Dowd that involves a girl forming a punk band with her teen cousins. I was so excited to have such a cool and substantial part. My first job, in *Foxes*, had been just a couple of scenes. I thought it would be an incredible opportunity and a lot of fun, especially because I loved music.

Real musicians are in the film, including some even an eighth grader would have known at the time—Steve Jones and Paul Cook of the Sex Pistols, Paul Simonon of The Clash, and Fee Waybill of the Tubes. I was very young, so my mother fought me on taking the job, but eventually I won. She felt better once she arranged to have a responsible girlfriend of hers stay with me for the whole shoot and play mama bear on set.

I left at the beginning of eighth grade to do the movie, and I had my thirteenth birthday a month into filming. It was a pretty radical experience on a lot of levels. I remember when I showed up on set, I had long, blond Alice in Wonderland hair down to my elbows. The hairstylist gave me a pixie cut with a tail and dyed it black, then bleached the top and down the middle, skunk like.

Having my identity as a long-haired, innocent girl completely altered was my first experience of becoming a different person on-screen. And even though I had a guardian, I saw plenty in the realm of sex and drugs. Who would have thought that the set of a movie featuring the Sex Pistols would be the place where a kid would decide to never do drugs? I saw people shaking from withdrawal and walked into rooms where cocaine was sitting out, and I found it all very confusing.

Being exposed to too much too young led to a healthy terror for me. Ironically, Paul and Steve were protective of and honest with me about drug use and the heartbreak that it had caused them. They'd just lost Sid Vicious to an overdose.

When I returned to eighth grade with my short hair, having witnessed some real-life shit, the class was reading *The Diary of Anne Frank* out loud. As one girl came to the line about Anne getting her period, everyone started giggling, and the girl blushed. I just rolled my eyes. I couldn't relate to middle schoolers anymore in their innocence. After what I'd seen and experienced on the *Stains* set, returning to school and to my mom's home, I didn't feel like a kid anymore.

MARIN KANTER, DIANE LANE, AND LAURA, *LADIES AND GENTLEMEN, THE FABULOUS STAINS*

BRUCE AND DIANE, *THE WILD ANGELS*

WALK

THE
ANGELS' FAULT

DIANE: You look nervous. Are you scared to ask something?

LAURA: A little.

DIANE: It's now or never, Laura. What do you want to know?

LAURA: Well… I realize that I avoid certain questions because I never want to hurt you and it must be hard to talk about, but I've always wondered—how did you become pregnant with my sister?

DIANE: Oh.

LAURA: Is that OK to ask?

DIANE: Of course. I'll tell you if you really want to know. Your father and I met doing *Orpheus Descending*.

LAURA: Didn't you actually meet onstage?

DIANE: Yes. After we'd moved to Off Broadway, the male lead had gotten another part and was leaving our show. A promising young actor, Bruce Dern, who'd already done two Broadway shows and had some good reviews, replaced him. And…you might say *Orpheus* descended!

LAURA: Oh, Mom! [*Laughs.*] That was the detail I remembered: that you met on-stage, in front of an audience! That's so crazy.

DIANE: But it was far from love at first sight. I had a monologue at the opening of the play. You've got to get the audience right away, and I got my audience every night. Except when Bruce comes in, suddenly I feel my audience's attention shifting. What was wrong? I look behind me at the corner of the store set. Bruce is over there looking through shoeboxes while I'm doing my monologue. After the curtain call, I cornered him backstage, and I said, "Boy, you better listen to me. When I'm on that stage doing my monologue, you do nothing. Do you hear me? You don't *move* on that stage when I'm doing my monologue. Do you hear me, Bruce Dern?" He said, "Oh, all right." I said, "I mean it. I'll come after you right onstage if you do that again. Don't you *dare*." That's how we started.

LAURA: So how did you wind up dating?

DIANE: Well, I was about to take off and let my understudy do the part for a while because I was trying out for this other Broadway play, *Weekend with Feathers*.

LAURA: Right. What was the play about?

Tal-Enge
INTERIORS

FURNITURE FOR GRACIOUS LIVING . . .
BED ROOMS · LIVING ROOMS · DINING
ROOMS · STEREO-HI-FI-WALL UNITS

FREE PARKING
OPEN DAILY 9:30 TO 7 P.M.
MON. - THURS. TILL 9 P.M.
326 FIFTH AVENUE
NEW YORK 1, N. Y.
MU. 5-3720-1

STELLA HOLT and **AL LIEBERMAN**

present

ADRIAN HALL'S

production of

TENNESSEE WILLIAMS'

ORPHEUS DESCENDING

with

Bruce **DERN**   Maggie **OWENS**   Diane **LADD**   Sylvia **DAVIS**

Directed by
ADRIAN HALL

Set and costumes by
ROBERT SOULE

Lighting by
LEWIS STEEL

Production coordinated by
JOHN TAYLOR

Giuseppe Sardi
FLORENTINE CUISINE

COCKTAILS

SEAFOOD
"Cacciucco" special
de Lla Casa
STEAKS AND
CHOPS SCALLOPINE

360 West 42 St. (off 9th Ave.)
LOngacre 5-9214

Open Daily
till 2 A. M.

RESTAURANT

THE
MANDARIN
HOUSE

AUTHENTIC MANDARIN-STYLE
CHINESE FOOD

*Luncheon -
Dinner - Supper;*
COCKTAILS

Open Daily Noon to Midnight
NO! NO CHOP SUEY!
*American
Express*

133 WEST 13TH ST.   WA 9-0551

ORPHEUS DESCENDING PLAYBILL

"BEAUTIFUL"
—Atkinson, N.Y. Times

"IMPECCABLE"
—Kerr, Herald Tribune

"STIRRING"
—Lewis, Cue

ANTON CHEKHOV'S

The Three Sisters

Tues., Wed., Thurs., Sun. Eves. 8.40 & Sun. Mat.
at 3:00, $2.50, 3.55, 3.90, Fri. Eves. 8.40 &
Sat. Eves. at 7:00 and 10:15, $3.90 & 4.60

4th St. Theatre   83 East 4th St. · AL 4-7954

The ARTS CAFE

Relaxed Continental Atmosphere

Serving Delicious
• ESPRESSO   • PASTRIES
• ICE CREAMS   • ITALIAN ICES
• SOFT DRINKS   • TEAS
      • SANDWICHES

SCULPTURE AND PAINTINGS FOR SALE

Next to
GRAMERCY ARTS THEATRE

140 E. 27th ST.

The Lichee Tree

荔
枝
樹

Leisure Luncheon
Business Lunch
Dinner
Chinese Banquet

COCKTAIL LOUNGE

OPEN EVERY DAY
Orders to Take Home

Catering Service

65 East 8th St.   GR 5-0555

NEW YORK'S NEWEST
JAZZ GALLERY
"Showcase for Modern Jazz"
80 ST. MARK'S PLACE
8th Street near First Avenue

Jazz Gallery

NEW YORK'S NEWEST
JAZZ GALLERY
"Showcase for Modern Jazz"
80 ST. MARK'S PLACE
8th Street near First Avenue

Synopsis of Scenes

The action of the play takes place in a general drygoods store and part
of a connecting "confectionery" in a small southern town, during the
rainy season, late winter and early spring.

ACT I

Scene 1 Late dusk.
Scene 2 A couple of hours later that night.

Intermission

ACT II

Scene 1 Afternoon, a few weeks later.
Scene 2 Late that night.

Intermission

ACT III

Scene 1 Early morning the Saturday before Easter
Scene 2 Sunset, the same day.
Scene 3 A half hour later.

THE CAST
in order of appearance

DOLLY HAMMA	Katherine Helmond
BEULAH BINNINGS	Essie Jane Coryell
PEE WEE BINNINGS	Charles Armsby
DOG HAMMA	Martin J. McCarrick
CAROL CUTRERE	Diane Ladd
EVA TEMPLE	Dorothy Dill
SISTER TEMPLE	Marie Fyrer
VAL XAVIER	Bruce Dern
VEE TALBOTT	Sylvia Davis
LADY TORRANCE	Maggie Owens
JABE TORRANCE	Robert Buzzell
SHERIFF TALBOTT	Houghton Jones
DAVID CUTRERE	Crayton Rowe
NURSE PORTER	Jimmie Duncan

Contemporary Paintings

by important name artists

AT AMAZINGLY LOW COST

A COLLECTOR'S PARADISE

THE ART FAIR

127 2nd AVE., (7th ST.) N.Y.C.

OREGON 4-6545

Open daily and Sunday 12-6
Closed Mondays

Epatez le bourgeois..

ALEXANDER KING
READS FROM HIS
BEST SELLER
and other stories

Mine Enemy
Grows Older

available at
your record
dealer

URANIA
UX-120

"HILARIOUS!"
—McClain, Jrl. Amer.

"RANKS WITH THE BEST!"
—Aston, W. Tele. & Sun

JERRY HERMAN'S

PARADE

the hit musical revue

DODY GOODMAN

with RICHARD TONE

PLAYERS THEATRE
115 Macdougal St., Al. 4-5076

Tues., Wed., Thurs. at 8-40 & Sun. at 3:60 and
8:40: $4.50, 3.90, 2.60, 3r. at 8-40 & Sat. at
7:30 and 10:30, $4.85, 4.50, 3.90, (tax included)

Who's Who

BRUCE DERN
(Val Xavier)

Mr. Dern, who hails from Winnetka, Ill., is the nephew of Archibald MacLeish and a grandson of George Henry Dern, a former governor of Utah and Secretary of War during F.D.R.'s administration. When he decided to making acting his career, he auditioned for and was accepted by the Actors' Studio where he was seen by Jules Garfein who cast him in "Shadow of a Gunman." Immediately following the closing of this play, Elia Kazan cast him as Rip Torn's understudy in "Sweet Bird of Youth." Kazan also selected him for an important role with Montgomery Clift in the forthcoming film, "Swift River."

MAGGIE OWENS
(Lady Torrance)

Miss Owens most recently appeared on tour in "Sweet Love Remembered." starring the late Margaret Sullivan and among her credits number "Epitaph for George Dillon" in St. Louis, and the role of "Lady" in the Hampden Theatre, New Hampshire, production of "Orpheus Descending". Off-Broadway, she also appeared in "Eastward in Eden," "Right You Are If You Think You Are," and "Ardele." She is the wife of WMCA's Disc Jockey, Joe O'Brien.

DIANE LADD
(Carol Cutrere)

At 17, Miss Ladd toured in Tobacco Road with John Carradine. She was seen in the national company of "A Hatful of Rain" with Ben Gazarra. Hailing from Lumberton, Mississippi, the former Copa Girl has appeared on most major TV series including "The Walter Winchell File", "The Big Story" and "Naked City" co-starring with Eugenie Leontovich. Recently she was the subject of a photo-article in "T.V. Guide". She was last seen on TV starring in the "Victor Riesel Story".

SYLVIA DAVIS
(Vee Talbot)

Miss Davis recently trouped the country in the national company of "Middle of the Night" with Edward G. Robinson. She was featured with the Lunts in "The Great Sebastians" and as Linda Loman in the national company of "The Death of a Salesman". In the original T.V. production of "Visit to a Small Planet" with Cyril Ritchard, she created the role of the mother.

ESSIE JANE CORYELL
(Beulah Binnings)

Miss Coryell has appeared in more than 200 plays in New York, on tour and in summer stock. Last season she was seen in the off-Broadway production of "On The Town." Among the plays and musicals she has appeared in are "Tobacco Road," "Claudia," "Carousel," "Call Me Madam," "Annie Get Your Gun."

ROBERT BUZZELL
(Jabe Torrance)

Mr. Buzzell is a graduate of the Pasadena Playhouse. He has several years of summer stock to his credit in Ogunquit, Maine, and Nantucket, Mass. This past year he was associate producer and actor at the Mt. Kisco Summer Theatre. He has been active with industrial shows on tour.

KATHERINE HELMOND
(Dolly Hamma)

Miss Helmond is working under Stella Holt's auspices for the second season, having last served her in "Trip to Bountiful" at Theatre East. She has also appeared in Equity Library Theatre productions of "Time of Your Life" and "Another Part of the Forest".

HOUGHTON JONES
(Sheriff Talbott)

A graduate of the American Academy, Mr. Jones was road manager and actor with the Michael Chekhov Theatre. He also acted with the Ashland, Oregon Shakespeare Festival and for many years served as director of community theatres in Utica, New York and Portland, Oregon.

DOROTHY DILL
(Eva Temple)

Miss Dill's initial stage bow was in the Masque Players production of "Rebecca". An alumnus of Madame Piscator's Dramatic Workshop, she has appeared in the Blackfriar Guild's productions of "Truce of the Bear" and "Child of the Morning".

MARIE FURER
(Sister Temple)

Has played a wide range of character roles in stock at Cape May, N.J. and Orleans, Mass. Off Broadway she was seen in PILLARS OF SOCIETY at the Cherry Lane, in ITALIAN STRAW HAT, at the Fourth Street Theatre and in COMRADES at the Royal Playhouse.

CRAYTON ROWE
(David Cutrere)

A student of Mildred Dunnock, Mr. Rowe has appeared in several of her productions at the Minor Latham Playhouse including "The Fantastics" and "Time Of Your Life". He was also featured in Arthur Miller's "View From The Bridge" at the St. Marks Playhouse.

CHARLES ARMSBY
(Pee Wee Binnings)

A native of Texas, he has appeared at nearly all the theatres in his home town of Houston. He has just completed a successful stock season where he played a wide variety of roles in such perennials as STALAG 17, THE RELUCTANT DEBUTANTE, and THE MOON IS BLUE.

MARTIN J. McCARRICK
(Dog Hamma)

Mr. McCarrick made his acting debut in "The Lower Depths" at the Contemporary Theatre in New York. He has also worked with the New York Shakespeare Festival.

STELLA HOLT
(Producer)

Stella Holt has been in continuous production off-Broadway since 1952. She has twenty-two productions to her credit including such hits as "Me, Candido", "A Land Beyond The River" and "Simply Heavenly" which went from off-Broadway to Broadway. Her permanent base of operations is the Greenwich Mews Theatre. She is the proud possessor of the much coveted rights to Jules Romain's world-famous "Dr. Knock" which she will produce later this season.

AL LIEBERMAN
(Producer)

Al Lieberman—better known as "Judge Lieberman"—resides in Weehawken, N.J. where he served as Judge of the Municipal Court for many years. He is a Founder of the Albert Einstein College of Medicine of Yeshiva University and is presently serving as its New Jersey chairman; served for past ten years as New Jersey chairman of the United Jewish Appeal and is also chairman of the Planning Committee of the Friars Club. He recently organized a Foundation to give scholarships to deserving students desirous of studying in colleges and for the theatre.

ADRIAN HALL
(The Director)

Adrian Hall has been represented off-Broadway by "The Trip to Bountiful", "Journey With Strangers" and "The Long Gallery". He has directed Equity Library Theatre productions of "Another Part of the Forest", "The Time of Your Life" and "Orpheus Descending". It was his direction of this last play at the Equity Library Theatre which moved playwright Tennessee Williams to grant the rights for this off-Broadway production, with the stipulation that Mr. Hall direct.

JOHN TAYLOR
(Production Co-ordinator)

Equally adept in the acting and production ends of the theatre, Mr. Taylor made his New York bow in Stella Holt's production of "The Long Gallery" shortly after serving as production manager for "An Evening with Oscar Wilde". He most recently played a season of repertory with the Pittsburgh Miniature Theatre.

LEWIS M. STEEL
(Production Manager & Lighting Director)

Graduated from Harvard University Class of '58, Mr. Steel has just completed a six month tour as assistant stage manager of a production of "Babes in Arms". He previously had directed Harvard theatre groups and a production of "The Lark" at the San Antonio Little Theatre.

HOWARD LONDON
(Stage Manager)

This is the fourth Adrian Hall-directed off-Broadway production which Mr. London has stage managed, the others being "The Long Gallery", "Trip to Bountiful" and "Journey With Strangers". He has also worked with Tallulah Bankhead, Eve Arden and Mae West.

STAFF

STAFF FOR ORPHEUS DESCENDING

GENERAL MANAGER	Stella Holt
ASSISTANT TO THE PRODUCERS	Diane Ladd
PRODUCTION MANAGER	Lewis Steel
PRODUCTION STAGE MANAGER	Howard London
TECHNICAL DIRECTOR	Frank Meottel
PRESS REPRESENTATIVES	Karl Bernstein and Ben Kornzweig
ASSOC. PRESS REPRESENTATIVE	Bob Ganshow
ADVERTISING	Lawrence Weiner & Associates
PROMOTION ASSISTANT	Jeremiah O'Connell
PRESS ASSISTANT	Lawrence Witchel
PHOTOGRAPHERS	Avery Willard, Roland Van Zandt
LEGAL CONSULTANT	Arthur Greenidge
HOUSE MANAGER	Joseph D. Antonelli
BOX OFFICE MANAGER	Maurice Scheded
PRODUCTION CONSULTANT	Lawrence Olvin
STAFF TECHNICIAN	Thomas Ravick
SCENERY EXECUTED BY	Sigurd Lomaki
LIGHTING OPERATOR	David Enke
PRODUCTION ASSISTANTS	Debra Cole, William Schroeder

Playgram is published by The Wilmore Playgram, Incorporated, 406 Broad Avenue, Palisades Park, New Jersey. Telephone Windsor 7-1423; in New York call Wisconsin 7-9132. All rights reserved. Reproduction without permission of any material contained herein is prohibited.

DIANE: A prostitute. Knowing *nothing* about prostitution, I knew I needed to do some research. So who to ask? I asked my costar. He said, "You want to see one on the move now?" I said, "Sure!" And your father was thinking, "Oh, whoa! This girl is a wild, open person!" And here I am, still this naive Mississippi Catholic girl. And so he takes me to this fairly elegant all-night restaurant with tables, booths, and a counter. He whispers to me that we should sit at the counter so we can see all the action. It's about one thirty in the morning, after our play was over. We order a piece of pie. We're sitting at a counter, and way at the other end of the counter is this guy, looks like a nice businessman, sitting alone. I said, "This is no place where hookers come!" But your daddy knew. Sure enough, here comes a really cute woman. She sidles up next to the other guy and orders a cup of tea, and she's putting the make on him, right in front of my eyes, and I'm getting to watch this whole thing. The funny part is your daddy thought I was so open-minded, when I was just trying to focus on my work, find out how to play this part. Still, I guess he got it into his head that I might be a little wild. So a week later, on our night off, he invited me out to see his home in New Jersey. It was nothing like a place I thought that Bruce would live! He had been married before for a couple of years and wound up staying in the all-American suburban house they'd lived in together.

LAURA: Fascinating.

DIANE: Yep. We had dinner, and we lay on the floor and listened to beautiful classical music. Lying there, I thought that your father was the loneliest man I had ever met. My heart just went out to him as a human being. He was the third child of John Dern, a powerful attorney. Of course, I suppose you know that your dad's paternal grandfather was governor of Utah and secretary of war under Roosevelt.

LAURA: Yes, but go on. I like hearing you talk about it.

DIANE: His maternal great-grandfather came over from Scotland and worked diligently to form and build a dry goods store that became one of the country's most successful department stores, while his great-grandmother formed a major prep school, two colleges, and wrote five books. One of their sons, his great-uncle, was the poet Archibald MacLeish.

LAURA: Right. I know.

DIANE: They weren't born with a silver spoon. They made and polished that spoon. And by the time your father came along, they were a very successful and well-respected family. People always thought your father was the country boy and that

I was the society girl. But it was the other way around, actually, if you go by our backgrounds.

LAURA: OK, so back to your date.

DIANE: Yes, there I am in your dad's suburban house after our strange prostitute-spotting date. Now, Laura, you've asked me about this before, and I haven't told you, so here's the truth! Why not? We do a little kissing on the floor. Then I said, "I have to go to bed." It was too late for me to go home, so I was going to stay over in the other room. So he goes to his room and I go to mine. Now he gets up to go get some water or something and passes my door. Laura, I swear to God, I really think the angels pushed against my door and opened it! Because I had closed it! He saw me, slightly bending over and slowly undoing my garter belt that came up to midthigh and removing my stockings slowly so as not to rip them. In those days, we young ladies wore a garter belt with hose. Apparently, to him, it was a rather arousing act. Again, I swear to you, I was totally unaware that I had an audience! But your dad really thought that I was doing this for him! He was fantasizing, *Oh my God, she knows I'm passing her and she's doing that move to turn me on.*

LAURA: Well, if you really weren't interested, you would have closed your door tighter.

DIANE: Laura! By God, I did not know that damn door was open, Laura! And I'm telling you, my angels pushed that door open. So help me God—they pushed that door open, and they said, "Take off your stockings!" I was set up by my own angels!

LAURA: OK, Mom! Your angels opened your door and made you take your sexy stockings off in a sexy way! Fine!

DIANE: I'm telling you true. Bruce came back and knocked on the door and said, "I brought you a cup of tea." By now I had my gown on. And he came in and was so sweet, and he moved in on me with charm. That's all it took! Honey, I was gone! I decided: *I am going to have sex with him.* I said, "If we're going to sleep together, we have to use protection. I don't want to get pregnant." He said, "You don't have to worry about that. I can't have children. My ex-wife and I tried. They've tested me. I'm sterile."

LAURA: Are you serious? He was lying! *Dad!* That's outrageous!

DIANE: No, he wasn't lying. They really tried to have a child! They went to doctors! Bruce was told that he was sterile and could not get anyone pregnant. So I slept with your daddy one time, Laura, and bam, I was pregnant! Months later, his ex-wife came to pick up an old lamp of hers that we had. When I opened the door, she saw my stomach. She gave me this dirty look and said, "You know, Bruce can't have children. He's sterile!" I replied, "If Bruce is sterile, you're looking at the Holy Virgin Diane!" So, Laura, you tell me how this couple tries for two years steadfastly but unsuccessfully to get pregnant! Then this little lady shows up, and wham, bam, thank you, ma'am, I'm pregnant in one hit!

LAURA: I don't know, maybe it's the power of Diane's angels.

DIANE: Oh, you're too much, Laura. No, it was the hand of God.

LAURA: Hmm, Mom, maybe you're right and God had something to do with it, but I think it had a lot to do with your, I don't know, *having sex*?

DIANE: It wasn't planned, but it was meant to be! All I know is that the angels were preparing me to have my children!

LAURA: OK, Mom. So that's how you had my sister. And tell me again where I was conceived. Wasn't it on the set of *The Wild Angels*?

DIANE: Well, it was when we were making that movie. Roger Corman directed, and it starred Peter Fonda and Nancy Sinatra. It opened the Venice Film Festival that year.

LAURA: What I heard from Dad was that you had been struggling for a long time to conceive, and then all the bouncing on the back of the Harley must have "shaken an egg loose" or something.

DIANE: Oh dear! I don't believe that at all. That sounds like a Bruce Dern story.

LAURA: Well, all I know is, Roger Corman likes to say, "If it weren't for me, Laura Dern wouldn't have been born!"

DIANE: That is funny. All I know is that Laura Dern was supposed to come here to planet Earth, having chosen Bruce Dern and Diane Ladd to be her parents! I absolutely believe that, honey, baby, mine. But now I'm tired. I'm really tired. *[Coughing fit.]* Hear that noise when I'm coughing? What even is that sound, you think? Is that the scarring, the reflux, or the infection?

LAURA: I don't know, Mom. But I do know that I need you to stick around for a long, long time. You have a lot more stories to tell me.

Diane

I was pregnant with Laura when I was doing a film called *The Rebel Rousers* with Harry Dean Stanton, Jack Nicholson, Cameron Mitchell, and Bruce Dern. We had to shoot in Kingman, Arizona, when I was eight months pregnant.

I was getting nervous that if something went wrong, I would need a caesarean. When we began shooting in Arizona, I asked, "Is there a good doctor here?" They said, "Yeah, we have a good ol' doctor—when he's sober." After that, every night, I just lay there and prayed to God, "Please get me and this baby off this set safely."

In one scene, the director had Harry Dean and Jack jumping up and down on the roof of the car I was in, trying to assault my character. The top of the car started to bend in. I jumped out of the car and screamed, "That's quite enough of that! I've got a baby in here!"

They were actually very chivalrous, though. At one point, Jack had to lean toward me menacingly and was very nervous about it. He said he didn't want to actually scare me.

When Harry Dean met Laura a few years later, he said, "I hope my voice isn't familiar to you." He worried that he'd made a bad impression when his character was trying to attack mine and she was along for the ride!

WALK

THE SEA IS WIDE

DIANE: How lovely to be strolling on Ocean Avenue in Santa Monica. There's no-where I'd rather be today.

LAURA: Did you know this is the tree that Jaya and Ellery would climb when they were little? We still come here sometimes to watch the sun set. This is our spot.

DIANE: Oh, I love that.

LAURA: And see that one limb being held up by that post?

DIANE: Yeah.

LAURA: That's the tree that Ellery took years to finally feel safe enough to climb. He jumped from it as though it was the scariest, furthest, hardest thing. What is that? Three feet up?

DIANE: Yeah.

LAURA: And now he'll jump off a twenty-foot cliff into the ocean without any fear! Did I ever tell you what Cheryl Strayed told Ellery about fear when he was little? One night Cheryl and I were on a hike in Northern California with Ellery. And there was something in the bushes, clearly a wild animal. And I was scared, but I was behind them, so Cheryl didn't see my fear. Ellery was walking next to Cheryl, and he heard this loud rustling and flinched. And Cheryl turned to him, and she said, "Ellery, are you going to let fear be your god or courage be your god?"

DIANE: Oh wow.

LAURA: He says he's never forgotten that moment.

DIANE: Wow. No wonder she's such a great writer.

LAURA: And friend. Anyway, now he's off to college in a few months, and I'm trying so hard not to have separation anxiety or to worry: to be on his own. I don't know. But it's not my job anymore to remind him to clean the house or to turn off the oven or not to leave a candle lit. I trust his choices, but how do you stop worrying?

DIANE: It is the hardest thing, letting go of your kids. And by the way, you never do.

LAURA: Ha, I just remembered that when I was a teenager, one of my friends, an-other young actress, called me very emotional, sobbing. I said, "What's wrong?" She said, "I went to my therapist crying and he diagnosed me. I have a diagnosis!" I said,

"What's your diagnosis?" She said, "Anticipatory nostalgia. Because I was crying thinking how sad I'll feel when my son goes away to college." She did not even have children yet. She was eighteen!

DIANE: I don't know how I let you move out at seventeen to go to UCLA. I guess it's because you were moving in with a family friend I trusted. I said, "You can't move out of my house unless you find a home that's as spiritual as our home." So you informed me that you were moving in with Marianne Williamson! When someone asked her, "Why are you letting a seventeen-year-old girl live in your home?" she said, "This seventeen-year-old has more sense than most grown-ups I know!" You wanted to fly, and I wanted to love you enough to let you fly.

LAURA: Staying with someone we knew was a safer option. If I was coming and going for work, it was going to be hard to be in a dorm. But then I started working so much, and UCLA wouldn't let me take a gap year. Do you remember? I got offered *Blue Velvet* two days into my first semester and asked to take eight weeks off to make the movie. I *begged* them. They said no. In that case, I said, how about a gap year? I gave them the script to read. Surely they'd see how important it was that I do that movie. They said: "Not only will you not get a gap year, but I can't believe you're saying goodbye to your college education over this." After I left, I wasn't allowed to come back at all!

DIANE: It was so stupid of them to not let you take a gap year. Talk about how the system grounds people instead of helping them fly.

LAURA: And you want to know the greatest irony? I've heard that if you want a master's degree in film from UCLA, one of the key movies you study and many have written a thesis on is *Blue Velvet*—a movie I got kicked out of that school for doing. I really wanted to go to college too!

DIANE: You got ticked off, and with good reason. You made the right choice, of course. When I first saw you up on the screen, I started to cry. So much talent! I thought to myself, *This child came through my body so that she could give her gift to the world and entertain people and teach them!* I had to find a balance between license and liberty. When you were a teenager, I made sure you had someone go with you to auditions and press.

LAURA: I'm really lucky that you chose savvy women to be around for me as a maternal figure while also giving me some autonomy from it being you. I would never let Jaya go off on location. I don't care if she had four nannies, I would never let her act until she was grown.

DIANE: That's unfair to the soul in your child's body! Everybody has a different path, and some start earlier, and it's your job to listen. Yes, protect, but encourage their gifts! And when you went to do *Ladies and Gentlemen, The Fabulous Stains* as a teenager, I had guards with you—trustworthy guards!

LAURA: One guard.

DIANE: One darn great guard!

LAURA: One good guard, for sure.

DIANE: Damn right.

LAURA: She ended up taking care of me and Diane Lane.

DIANE: Yeah. She took care of both of you. I was always praying for you every night and calling you. And I flew down to check on you.

LAURA: Yes, you did, with Grandma.

DIANE: Did I bring her along also?

LAURA: Yes, and you wore your favorite thing: that red sweatshirt nightgown that went to the floor. It zipped up the front and had little pockets and a hood. And you used to wear it with Dr. Scholl's sandals.

DIANE: Oh. Some memory, wow. My memory's not that good. I have an actor's memory. I could take a history book home and memorize the whole thing for a test and get an A the next day. But then after that, I forget everything I read. I can always learn lines, bam, on the way to the set. But if someone says, "I love that line you said in that movie!" I don't know what line they're talking about.

LAURA: Ha, well, that red outfit made an impression. Diane Lane loved it so much that you gave it to her when you left. And she wore it every night after that.

DIANE: Aw, bless her heart.

LAURA: I can't imagine what it was like for you when I went off to work when I was younger. I'm going to have a taste of that soon when Ellery goes off to college. I'm a little nervous about how I'll handle it.

DIANE: Well, it's a real transition you've got to face and to honor. When you left home, I knew you were working and learning, and that brought me a lot of joy. You can have joy and fear and all the emotions at the same time. You just need to look at the big picture of what you're accomplishing and why. Every time I missed you, I made myself think: *She is spreading her wings! She's learning to live her own life!* I was proud of your initiative. It was a great pride that I felt as a parent. I had accomplished something that I was supposed to accomplish. But it was a very hard time, feeling you pull away.

LAURA: When I was out on my own, from eighteen to twenty-five—those were the years that we fought the most. Is it going to be like that with my kids? What is that going to feel like? I think what I'm afraid of is not my own sadness about it but feeling lonely. I'm a single mom like you were, so the house is going to feel really empty when the kids are gone. What did you do to distract yourself?

DIANE: I tried to fill the space. You have to find other things to do. Do you like to sew?

LAURA: Me?

DIANE: Well, do you like to read? Do you like to paint? And maybe there's something you always wanted to do that you never tried. I started taking singing lessons and trying to take piano lessons and just anything that could take my mind and turn it in another direction.

LAURA: Do you remember relief in my leaving home? Was there any part, even if it was five percent, where you felt like, *Diane's life starts now!*

DIANE: No, your priority is still not yourself. You try to make it that. And you go off and you do things. But your need to care for that child is there every minute. It never leaves—never, Laura! That's why there are couples who raise their children and are happy together until the birds fly away, and then the two people look at each other and say, "We don't have anything to talk about." There's a vacancy, an emptiness, a hole. It was very hard for me at first. I had good friends, but I wasn't married at the time, and I was very, very lonely. You were my life, my heart. Even now, I always want to know that you're OK. [*Cries.*]

LAURA: I know how you feel, Mom...truly. What's the expression—"A mother is only as happy as her saddest child"? We pour it all into this person. Then they grow up. Wow.

DIANE: I know. It's so beautiful, and, man, it can just be hell.

LAURA: Both at once. The burden and the bliss. And that goes both ways. When I was young and you were away working, I felt separation anxiety from you too.

DIANE: Do you feel like I screwed you up?

LAURA: Uh. Absolutely.

DIANE: Wait a minute, you've got a rough look on your face.

LAURA: Maybe we don't need to look back—regrets don't always serve, right?

DIANE: It's OK if you send me sobbing and running away. I can take it!

LAURA: Are you sure you want to go there?

DIANE: I can take it, Laura.

LAURA: You really want to hear what I have to say? OK. Well, to start with, I guess I wish you hadn't been so reactive.

DIANE: I bet you're thinking of the time I slapped you.

LAURA: Yeah. That's one of my least favorite memories.

DIANE: It's indefensible, but in my defense you were being bratty.

LAURA: In other words, it's *not* indefensible.

DIANE: You mouthed off to me, and I'd had a horrible day. The shock of your mouthing off to me just sent me spinning. I couldn't believe it. You were only ten, and you said something really teenage-smart at the refrigerator. I'll never forget it. I hated myself for it, and I thought, *What am I doing wrong as a parent? How could she talk to me like that?* I was devastated.

LAURA: Well, Mom, I appreciate you acknowledging that happened, because that's actually a big memory for me. But instead of saying you were devastated that you slapped me, you said you were devastated that you had a daughter who would talk back, so it's still my fault. Then don't bring that shit up because it's not an apology...and I was "being bratty"? That's your explanation? Not only is that a cop-out, Mom, but I didn't know that my childlike behavior was responsible for making you inappropriate. I'm not holding that anymore.

DIANE: OK. [*Deep breath.*] Let's try it differently. What do you remember?

LAURA: First of all, I wasn't ten—I was fourteen.

DIANE: I don't believe that. I remember you standing by the refrigerator looking *up* at me. By eleven, you were tall!

LAURA: Mom, I *was* fourteen—

DIANE: You *never* let me win an argument!

LAURA: And what I remember is you cussed at me and called me an awful name and went on about how I was letting you down not doing all the chores you wanted me to do. You called me selfish. And I said, very dramatically, "Like mother, like daughter," and you slapped me. It was so hard-core. I think you were really unhappy at work and wanted to come home and blame someone else.

DIANE: I guess I just snapped. Money worry, work stress, child support, all kinds of resentments. I was very angry and I took it out on you, and that's the truth. And I am sorry.

LAURA: Thank you for that. I will also say that it messed me up you always calling me your "miracle." It felt embarrassing and was an incredibly awkward label to carry or live up to. And it did not give room to just be me, whoever me is.

DIANE: Well, my mother was angry because she *hadn't* been her mother's focus! Her mother had eight children. Mary was the youngest and pissed off that her mother was tired and didn't seem to have enough time or energy for her. So I was Mary's focus, her doll, and my friends were her playmates. My daddy taught me gumption! Stand up for yourself and your beliefs! My mouth is louder because I did a lot of theater acting and I project easily! And I am southern, emotional, and a Sagittarian.

LAURA: That's a lot of reasons. You could just say, "Sorry."

DIANE: We all do something wrong. Give me just a second. Let's sit down on that bench.

LAURA: How about we walk a little more?

DIANE: Listen, I try to be loving. Someone treats me wrong and I hold it in and they push and push and finally I blow like a steam pot, like hell frosted over, and people don't expect that, you know? It's like, *What? Where'd that come from?* Of course, I'm the kind of person who, after I confront and blow up and tell you how I feel, I say, "You ready to go to the movie?"

LAURA: Yeah, exactly.

DIANE: But that's always true with everybody, isn't it?

LAURA: No. I mean, the person that blows up doesn't understand ten minutes later why the other person's still upset. Because you don't know how the attack feels. And that's been a big thing for me—learning how to say that I expect to be respected, regardless of someone's anger.

DIANE: Right. You are so right.

LAURA: It means a lot to hear it, Mom. I appreciate that. It was a hard time, and part of it was that you were gone a lot working and I missed you. I'm seeing it from the other side now with my own kids. I mean, at least you had Grandma Mary to help. I don't have that built-in grandma.

DIANE: I'm a built-in grandma.

LAURA: You're a working actor, which is gorgeous in a different way. That is inspiring to them, that you're still working and doing what you love.

DIANE: Ah. OK.

LAURA: They see a strong woman—

DIANE: It takes one to know one.

LAURA: Oh, let me finish.

DIANE: I will, but let me just say that because of my being a working mother, you got experiences that no kids get!

LAURA: I know. And we've talked about that before. And you've let me know how lucky I was a lot.

DIANE: Good.

LAURA: And I let my children know how lucky they are. But here's what we as women don't say to our children enough: "I felt so much pain being away from you. And I felt so guilty to leave. And it was so conflicted for me."

DIANE: I know you feel that way, sweetheart. But do you know what all you do for your children? You teach them about the world!

LAURA: But you know what? Here's the thing—

DIANE: You teach them love, Laura.

LAURA: I'm not saying this to hurt you, because you definitely let me know how loved I was. I did not have any experience of not knowing my mom loved me. And I know my kids know I love them. You and I—we're both loving mothers. But what I never said out loud was "I miss you. This is painful. I don't want you away from me." I feel like Jaya so wants to prove that she's a champion of women, and her grandma's such a badass that at eighty-five she's doing a movie and a TV series. And her mom's working and doing this important movie about mental health. And how amazing, and "I'm going to be like that when I grow up." But in a way it doesn't give her room for the other feelings, which are there too. And I didn't have room for that either. She should be able to say, and I should have said, "Mom, come home. I hate this." I never wanted to be the kid to make you feel bad for working, and I know Jaya has that too. But Jaya's having a rough time, and she deserves to express how *she* feels without me jumping in to try to make it better.

DIANE: Well, she's having a rough time, but I guarantee you so are the nineteen other kids in her class, including all of them whose families are home and not away for work.

LAURA: Mom, just let me say this one time, and then we can go back to explaining it away, all right? I was the child of a divorced family of working artists who were always traveling for their jobs, and sharing a home with a single actress mom. That had many benefits, and I was raised to believe that I could do anything. But this is also the truth: when you're a kid it hurts to be apart from your mother, and as a mother it hurts to be apart from your kid. I never told you how much it hurt, but I also never asked you how you felt, because I think you were working so hard to justify why it's always perfectly good—what great experiences I was having! Why it's important that you're making money! And how it's all fine because Grandma's there! But it's *painful*.

DIANE: [*Quietly.*] Yes, it is.

LAURA: I don't think I've ever really talked to you, Mom, about what it felt like to be lonely for you as a kid. And I think you created such wonderful distractions and the comfort in Grandma. I was always with a relative who loved me so fiercely. But still, when you were gone, it was painful. I think I never told you because you would remind me you were working because you loved it and you needed to make money. Grandma was supportive of you. I was trying to be very adult and not complain. But the truth is I really missed you. The time I remember missing you the most was after your second divorce.

DIANE: Yes, that was a really hard time.

LAURA: When you'd married Bill, we'd moved to New York together, and Grandma had stayed in LA, so I'd had those couple of years of just you and me. When that marriage ended, I was back in LA, and I think I felt a lot of anxiety. You were originating the role of Lu Ann Hampton Laverty Oberlander in *A Texas Trilogy* on Broadway.

I have such a strong memory of begging Grandma one night to call you. It was late for you. You had rehearsals the next morning. She explained that we couldn't call you, and that made me sadder to the point of being inconsolable. I was crying so hard I threw up. Then she did call you. And your voice immediately calmed me. You told me to get in your bed and cuddle up with my doll, Lucy, and the blanket we always snuggled in and have Grandma lay with me. And when I got into that position, you said we were going to say a poem together. I still don't know where you found it. You taught me to recite it with you.

The sea is wide

And you can't step it

And I love you

And you can't help it

And if you love me

Like I love you

Nothing

In the world

Can cut our love in two

From that time on, we always did that at bedtime. Wherever you were, you'd call to say good night, and we'd say the poem together.

Just so you know, Mom, now that I've shared that story with you and you're probably filled with guilt, know that I have the same amount going through me because I know I've done this to Jaya and Ellery, and I am tortured right now. I get it from both perspectives.

DIANE: OK. I want to come to that, but let me say that this badass working actress grandma is also the same grandma that lay on the grass with her granddaughter Jaya, lay on the grass on a blanket, and looked up at the sky, and she and I lay there, and looked at the universe, and talked—soul to soul, holding hands. The same way—

LAURA: But—

DIANE: Wait. The same way that you and I held hands in New York in the hotel the night that we lost Averil. We held hands laying side by side, and our souls were connected that night. Jaya told me later that stargazing was one of the best moments of her life with me. Now, I've tried to get back there many times, and it's always interrupted. Hell, I'm calling my grandchildren every night. They're too busy to call me back. But here's the thing, that badass grandma made that connection. And let me say this, on behalf of and in defense of our working as mothers, that my cousin back home, one of the sweetest people in the world, had five daughters. And if you think that there weren't times that she couldn't be with them, you're wrong. She wasn't off at work, but hell, she had a house to clean, and other children to diaper, and she had to get a meal on the table. You think there weren't times when she couldn't stop and be there for a child in need? She couldn't be there all the time either, Laura. And all of us, no matter what it is we're trying to do, go through this as mothers and fathers. The point is this, we by God cared.

LAURA: But—

DIANE: And we didn't do everything right, but that's just because we're only vulnerable human beings. I want to meet the person who does it all right. Maybe the Virgin Mary. Are we aspiring to be the Virgin Mary, Laura? Or are we just doing our best?

LAURA: What I'm doing now is trying to look at what I did wrong and change it, and it's a little late because Jaya's a sixteen-year-old. But at least I can be honest about how I feel about it—

DIANE: But you—

LAURA: I'm about to make a point, and you're—

DIANE: Sorry.

LAURA: —highlighting my point perfectly.

DIANE: Slap me.

LAURA: I would say, just like now, "What about the times when you weren't there for eight weeks?" And you're like, "But who took you to Europe? And who took you to meet spiritual leaders? And who…" Right?

DIANE: Yeah.

LAURA: I think our heartbreak about any mistakes is so great, and all I—

DIANE: It's because we love big, honey.

LAURA: I know. And all I'm trying to do, Mom, is to look, and I'm saying this with love because we have this extra time together. And you're in a marriage, and you have grandchildren, and you have these primary relationships. All we really can offer a loved one, when they bring up a negative, instead of going, "But you know what's amazing about that, actually?" is—

DIANE: You're right. We try to fix it instead of just listening.

LAURA: All we can really offer is just to sit with it. If Jaya says, "I'm so mad you're not here right now! I need you!" I have to remember not to say, "But remember, I'm home in two weeks. And you said you understood I needed to work, and I asked you if you wanted to come. And this will be good for us in so many ways…" I have to remember that what she wants to hear is, "I know. Doesn't this suck?" Or, frankly, I should just shut up and listen to her feelings.

DIANE: Yeah.

LAURA: I mean, fix it or don't. It's not always possible. I can't pull out of this movie at the last minute. But I can say, "Tell me how you feel." And I can just sit there and take it.

DIANE: You're right. It doesn't come naturally to me, but I need to do it. I need to just listen to you and take it. And say I am sorry I wasn't around more when you were young. I thought it was for the best, and I still do, but you're right, that doesn't mean there wasn't a cost. You don't care about the value of art at ten!

LAURA: You know, Mom, this is part of what I love so deeply about you. Even in your willingness to have these conversations, you're really not afraid of who you are. You're not afraid of facing the hard stuff. You understand that if you give me room to say what I feel, that it might be helpful to me. That's so cool.

DIANE: That's true, Laura. I just hate to think you were ever sad.

LAURA: I know. I feel the same way about Jaya. But let's be honest: parenting is always ultimately a mess. It's terrifying. It's complicated. All we want to do is do it differently than our parents did. And then I think back on when I was working, and Ben was on tour, and our babysitters Imelda and Marbelly were doing the fun part—just like Grandma Mary was with me when I was little. To be clear, they also did a hell of a lot of the hard work. I was so grateful for that help. They did so much for me and the kids, and they did it in such beautiful ways. Still, I found it hard to be away. I couldn't help worrying that I was missing important moments in their lives. I now know how that must have felt for you.

DIANE: Of course. No one's going to overshadow that bond that comes from a mother or a father. But at times I'd come home, and all I could think was, *Oh, look at that, my mother's having fun.* She was so proud when she divorced my father that she didn't take money from him. Oh, really? Well, you know what that means? Now your daughter has to pay your bills. You were too proud to take money from him, so he went and got married to somebody else and spent it on her, and now your daughter has to support you. Oh, isn't that wonderful that you're so proud? Didn't you do a wonderful thing that left me in this position? I mean, come on, Laura. You know what I'm talking about here. So, yes, of course I was pissed off that she's there with you having fun: "Curl my hair, Laura! Let's paint our toenails!" And I am working twelve-hour days making the money to pay the rent, buy her clothes, put food in her mouth for her to go get entertained and travel and play with you. I was the man of the house. You hear this whine in my voice?

LAURA: Yeah.

DIANE: Do you hear this child that hasn't grown up?

LAURA: I get it, Mom. I'm lucky that when I'm not shooting, I get to be home, and that I can afford help when I'm away, but even then, it can be so rough.

DIANE: You shouldn't feel guilty.

LAURA: Easy to say, but harder to feel. A therapist once said to me, "Your kids are fine. You continue to tell them you don't want to leave, and you feel so guilty. And so it's easy for them to start feeling like you think they can't handle it when you're gone. You should be letting them know that they're going to be fine and you're going to go make your art and make money for the family, and they know you'll be back."

DIANE: Listen to your therapist and to your mother: you need to stop feeling so guilty.

Laura

Now I feel bad that I gave my mom such a hard time about missing her and about slapping me when I was fourteen. She's going through so much, I don't need to make her feel guilty on top of it all. But it's the truth. And I'm sure it's Jaya's truth, and Ellery's. It's really painful to be little and away from your parents. This has been the downside for me of living an artistic life: an overwhelming guilt over being away from my kids. What consoles me is that the kids have grown up in a creative household. Ben's parents were musicians. Ellery's a born musician. He writes the most incredible lyrics. Jaya's signed up for every musical in school, and she's a gifted debater. I'd be just as happy if either of them wanted to be a politician or nurse, but I see our family's love of storytelling so powerfully coming through both of them. I definitely would never trade my lineage or my storytelling genetics for anything. I feel lucky and proud—even though I still feel awful about missing my kids, and when I was in their place it really sucked to be away from my mom.

ME, ELLERY, AND JAYA

LAURA AND BELLINA, AVERIL AND DIANE

9

MORNING
PHONE CALLS

LAURA: All last night I was thinking about what you said about the slap and how stressed out you were. I feel terrible bringing all that up. You have enough to deal with.

DIANE: No, that's what I'm here for right now. To hear these things.

LAURA: No, I need to say this: I'm an artist today because of you. I was able to see what it looks like to have a parent who loves her work and loves to inspire and be creative and tell stories. To do that, you had to be away. I'd rather have that example than have homecooked meals every night. You weren't there because you were paying our rent, you were doing what you loved, and you were surviving. And so you taught me how to do those things too, by your example. Mom, you're imperfect, but you're magnificent. And I was thinking today too of the greatest gift you gave me.

DIANE: What's that?

LAURA: Friends. You had such close friendships, and it made me realize that's what I wanted.

DIANE: You have always had such good friends. That's because you're such a great friend. I always tell people, "You'll never have a better friend than my daughter!"

LAURA: You too! We could never have dreamed of a better friendship than yours with Averil, which gave me my honorary sister, Bellina. From as long ago as I can remember, Averil was my aunt and you were Bellina's godmother, just like Bellina and I are now aunties to each other's children. It's amazing to think back on our mother-daughter life together and to think of almost no memory that doesn't include the two of them. God, Mom, so much is flooding my mind right now. Like when we spent summers with Averil and Bellina at the Malibu Outrigger condos.

DIANE: Those were wonderful times.

LAURA: You know, when I think about that scene in *Alice Doesn't Live Here Anymore* that we talked about earlier, where you and Ellen are sitting out in the parking lot, I think of you and Averil sitting side by side by the pool during those summer vacations in Malibu. All the single moms would sit by the pool with cocktails while the kids swam. Bellina and I would play mermaids all day and then we'd go to Dad's. You made our lives so fun.

DIANE: You were good company even as a little girl.

LAURA: I loved how Bellina and I could ask you and Averil anything. The conversations the four of us had when I was eight are almost as deep as the ones you and I are having now. You truly set an example for me in the value of friendship and how we shouldn't have to walk this life alone. And that we desperately need our deepest friends to bounce our decisions off of, to raise our kids with, to lean on for help. I don't know how empty my life would feel today if I hadn't seen your friendship with Averil as an example. You and she were really raising Bellina and me together. As two girls with single moms and her with much older siblings from another father, it felt like it was the two of us against the world. To be honest, I think I felt such guilt about ever telling you how much I wished I had a sibling. I never wanted to cause you or Dad pain in that way. But really I want to thank you for finding me one.

DIANE: That's right. Bellina was yours and Averil was mine.

LAURA: Mom, I need to tell you a memory that this has called up for me, one I'm starting to realize has shaped my whole life. I remember being eight at the Malibu Outrigger one morning. You woke up feeling inspired. You were in sweatpants and a T-shirt, looking out at the ocean, and you had an idea for a play. And that creative surge was so joyful for you. Bellina and I were supposed to go to my dad's, and you were meant to take us there. Mom, this makes me want to cry, remembering this with you. I watched you begin to shut down all of that inspiration to put on your armor and a little lipstick so that you looked decent in front of your ex and his new wife—you sort of didn't give a shit but also sort of did. You made sure to show me that everyone could get along even though they couldn't. You let me know that I was your priority, not just the need to be creative that day. And I remember so strongly Averil walking in and saying, "Nope! You're not changing out of those sweats. And you're not seeing your ex-husband this morning. You're going to follow your idea. You're allowed to give yourself your creativity as a present today. I'll take the girls. We'll get pancakes. And we'll see Bruce. And you'll have this time for yourself." What I remember most is seeing a mother honoring herself as an artist, as a deserved priority. I think that's kept me going instead of just saying, "Your kids are going through a divorce! You can't work! You can't be away from them!" I had to make money, and they deserved to feel what I felt watching Averil take care of you that day at the Outrigger condos. I wanted my kids to see their mom sometimes make herself a priority. And what I remember most is at the end of the day we came back, and you seemed so full. And so happy. And so available to me. The four of us played in the pool and took a walk on the beach and had dinner. And together we watched *Now, Voyager*, the Bette Davis movie. You seemed happy. And that made me so happy. It taught me to acknowledge that I need creativity—not just because it pays the rent but because it gives me room to show myself and my kids me at my most fulfilled.

DIANE: That's beautiful, honey. And you have no idea how happy it makes me.

LAURA: And Bellina is still built into the fabric of my life. She's in my most important decisions and my most mundane tasks. As are Dalia and Mandy. We have that middle school/high school sisterhood. And you taught me to keep those friends close my whole life. Like you did with yours. But you also made sure to teach me to stay open to the sisters I would find along the way. And I would say most days I'll have my morning coffee FaceTime with Reese to talk through what our kids are going through that day and how we should handle it, and every Sunday you know we're at Courteney Cox's for family dinner to cook and laugh and play pool. It's beautiful. Kids are running around. Courteney and I have spent every Christmas Eve morning with the kids since they were little. And I never feel alone. I have that in my life because of you, Mom. Even though I didn't grow up with siblings, you made me see that I could create my own family of sisters. When I was single again and going through a divorce, finding my role parenting in a house with the kids, I leaned into those friendships with Reese and Courteney, as well as Jayme and Mary . . . all my Southern sisters, because they remind me of you and Grandma. And I also have my other deep girlfriends too who have been my home base. I have all of these sisters because you set that example.

DIANE: My friends kept me going after you left home. You'll see with your kids gone. Your friends will be there for you when the loneliness hits.

LAURA: I believe you're right. When Kelly Preston died last year, I was so heartbroken. I loved her so much. Her death was a wake-up call for me. I wished I'd had more time with her. You've got to somehow stay in touch with people you love. I immediately started trying to get back in touch with friends I'd lost touch with.

DIANE: I loved Kelly too. And what a wonderful actress. I was lucky to direct her in *Mrs. Munck*. I love that adorable photo of the two of you napping together on the set of *Citizen Ruth*.

LAURA AND KELLY PRESTON NAPPING BETWEEN SCENES, *CITIZEN RUTH*

Your friends are your family. One of my great teachers, C. C. Bateman—one of Pappy Boyington's renowned Black Sheep flyers—said, "If you can even count your friends on one hand, you are very lucky, because your friend is your true diamond, and to have one or more makes you a very rich person." Friendships like the ones you have with Bellina and all those amazing women are what's going to see you through whenever you have trouble, or when you miss the kids after they leave home. I'm so relieved that you have people like her in your life. If I'm honest, it makes me less worried about dying, knowing that you have so much love and support.

LAURA: Mom, I love you so much. You look like you're getting tired. Let's go just to the end of the block, just a little bit more. Then we'll take you back.

OCT • 73

OCT • 73

OCT • 73

"Mom, I need to tell you a memory that this has called up for me, one I'm starting to realize has shaped my whole life."

—LAURA

BELLINA, DIANE, AND LAURA, ROYAL PREMIERE OF *RAMBLING ROSE*

Laura

My oldest and best friend is Bellina Logan. Both of us had dads who weren't around as much as our moms. Bellina's father was off with the Negro Ensemble Company and then teaching at Howard University. Bellina's mom, Averil Logan, was an English playwright who was at the Actors Studio at the same time as my parents. She'd written a play and asked my mom to be in it. When they began working on it, they realized they were both single mothers raising daughters who were just a few months apart in age, so they got us together.

For our first meeting, her nanny, Betty, who was like her grandma, and my Grandma Mary took us to El Coyote. Bellina dumped a bowl of guacamole over my head. So began the great sisterhood.

Bellina has two older sisters from her mother's previous marriage, but her sisters were twelve and fourteen years older, so she and I became like each other's sister. If I'm sick, she brings over food. She is my mom's godchild, as I was Shelley's.

People often see children growing up as the only kid in the house as lonely or isolated, but what I've found is that many of us find our own honorary siblings in time. I've got my own small army of sisterlike friends, and Bellina's is the longest friendship of all.

Bellina inspires me beyond measure, especially in how good a daughter she was to her mother. She walked Averil through Alzheimer's with such respect and thoughtfulness.

When her mother had to go into a home, Bellina re-created her bedroom in this facility and planted her favorite kind of bougainvillea in the window box so she'd see the same color out the window that she always had. She found a stuffed animal that looked like her mom's cat she'd loved best, so her mother could cuddle it at the home. She made a mixtape of her mother's favorite wartime big band songs and had it playing for her at all times. She stocked the room with her mother's favorite English chocolates. And every evening at five, she'd stop by to make Averil a martini. She did all this while raising a young child. I aspire to have a fraction of her kindness and grace.

Easy, *new way to make delicious*
BANANA PUDDING

ARABELLE JELL-WELL SAYS: You'll love *this extra-special, no-bake dessert!*

Crunchy-good Jane Arden Vanilla Wafers and rich, ripe bananas...smothered in the smooth, delicate *hand-blended* flavor of Jell-well Vanilla Pudding and Pie Filling. Such a spectacular dessert, you'd never dream it could be so quick, so easy to make. Get Jane Arden Vanilla Wafers and Jell-well Pudding and Pie Filling when you shop, today. Enjoy this treat tonight!

RECIPE
(MAKES 4-6 SERVINGS)

Prepare 1 package Jell-well Vanilla Pudding and Pie Filling according to package directions. Allow filling to cool. (If you prefer, use Jell-well Vanilla Instant Pudding, prepared according to package directions).

Line bottom and sides of low 9" square dish with Jane Arden Vanilla Wafers. Cover wafers with banana slices. Pour half of pudding over bananas. Add second layer of Jane Arden Wafers, bananas and remaining pudding. Chill about 1 hour. (For an extra-special touch, top with whipped cream sprinkled with crushed vanilla wafers — or use meringue topping and brown lightly).

Get a box of each, today!

Copyright 1956,
Jell-well Dessert Co.
Los Angeles, California

WALK

10

BANANA PUDDING
& RED WINE

LAURA: Sorry we're getting a late start. I had to take Jaya to guitar lessons.

DIANE: I can't believe Mary never gave me guitar or piano lessons.

LAURA: Well, you gave them to me. And I quit both. What do you want to talk about?

DIANE: Dealer's choice.

LAURA: OK, I thought we could do something a little lighter today. You know what I realized last night? When it comes to trivialities, I know so much more about my friends than I do about you. I know their favorite food, drink, song, book—all of it. I mean, I know Reese's favorite foods. But I don't know very many of those things about you. I *might* know your favorite drink—Chivas and soda. Am I right?

DIANE: Actually, yes. And there's a reason for that. It's because of an injury I got doing my first play on tour, *A Hatful of Rain*. I was so nervous that when I ran across the stage to jump up on a platform, I misjudged the landing and ripped a leg muscle really horribly. I was in a lot of pain, but I kept going until the curtain came down. Only then did I cry out. The doctor was going to give me a shot with a needle that was as long as my arm, but I said, "Don't give me that shot. What else can I do?" He said, "A shot of scotch?" And I did that. It took away the pain. Maybe that's why it—with some soda—became my favorite drink! I don't drink much more than one drink at a time. I don't like alcohol particularly. I have a martini about three times a year. Once in a while I have a margarita. I'll have a glass of wine with dinner and I never finish it. But if you have a toothache or you're tired, a good shot can pick you up.

LAURA: Do you know my favorite drink?

DIANE: No, what is it?

LAURA: Do you have any idea?

DIANE: What your favorite drink is?

LAURA: Yes.

DIANE: Scotch?

LAURA: No. I've never had scotch in my life.

DIANE: Bourbon whiskey.

LAURA: Never tasted bourbon, scotch, or whiskey. No. I like red wine.

DIANE: Well, that's a good one. You've got Jesus's first miracle going for you!

LAURA: Exactly. I'll stick with the blood and body of Christ. You know, I'm embarrassed to admit this, but I love the taste of communion wafers. I wish I could eat them as a snack.

DIANE: Laura Dern! You don't *snack on* the wafer!

LAURA: I just said I *wanted* to. Let's keep going. What's your favorite color?

DIANE: Well, I guess yellow, which I've heard called the color of wisdom. I think that's because it's the color of sunshine and symbolizes light shining on the darkness of ignorance.

LAURA: I would never have known that.

DIANE: And lavender, which, if you study chakras, is the color associated with the head chakra, and identified with self-knowledge.

LAURA: Well, I remember you loving lavender starting when you met your friend Glenda Christian. She would always wear that color.

DIANE: Yes, and so I did too, to be more like her. What's *your* favorite color, Laura? I think I know.

LAURA: I don't really have a favorite color. I would probably—

DIANE: Blue. Your favorite color has always been blue.

LAURA: No. I think my favorite color is probably the color of my couch, a salmon pink or dusty rose.

DIANE: Rose, like my given first name. That must be why it's your favorite color.

LAURA: Ha, yes, Mom, just like your name. You know, that reminds me of when I was pregnant with Jaya. Remember what you said?

DIANE: No, what?

LAURA: When I told you I was pregnant with a girl and said I had to figure out the right name for her, you said, "I've been thinking so hard about this. She needs to have her own thing, be an individual, and I have just the name. It's part of the family story, but it's her own independent, individual name." And I said, "That sounds great! What is it?" And what did you say?

DIANE: Diana.

LAURA: Diana. Your name with an *a*.

DIANE: Well, it is a very pretty name.

LAURA: Ha, I love that you thought an *a* just made it brand new and all hers!

DIANE: I did think so! And it made me think of Princess Diana, whom we loved!

LAURA: Remember she chose *Rambling Rose* for a royal premiere and we got to sit next to her and watch the film?

DIANE: Yes, of course! Anyway, then Jaya was born two hours before my birthday—it seemed like fate!

LAURA: I do like Laura for me. I think you guys nailed it. I know you said you loved Lara from *Doctor Zhivago*. Is that right?

DIANE: Yes.

LAURA: It feels strong. It's a girl's name, but there's nothing girly about it. There's room to grow into whoever you are and a fluidity to it that I appreciate. Isn't it funny that you have this responsibility to name this person you haven't met? If I'd been a boy, what would you have called me?

DIANE: Christopher Andrew. And we would have called you Drew.

LAURA: Ha, it's weird to think about being a Drew. Do you feel like you were given the right name?

DIANE: Yes, because I love Diana, goddess of the hunt. To choose my name, my mother put three names into a box: Charmaine, Jeanine, and Diane. I think I got the right one.

LAURA: OK, next! What is your favorite dessert?

DIANE: We have the same favorite there: banana pudding!

BANANA PUDDING

Prep Time 10 mins
Cook Time 20 mins
Total Time 30 mins

INSTRUCTIONS

INGREDIENTS

4 tablespoons all-purpose flour

1¾ cups sugar, divided

Pinch salt

3 large eggs, separated

3 cups milk

2 teaspoons vanilla extract, divided

1 box vanilla wafers
(approximately 45 wafers)

5–6 bananas, sliced

⅛ teaspoon cream of tartar

THE PUDDING

1. Preheat oven to 325°F.

2. In a large, heavy saucepan, combine flour, 1½ cups sugar, and salt.

3. In a large bowl or measuring cup, lightly beat egg yolks and combine with milk.

4. Pour egg mixture into dry ingredients. Cook over low-to-medium heat, stirring constantly, until ingredients are thickened and smooth.

5. Remove saucepan from heat and stir in 1 teaspoon vanilla.

6. Cover the bottom of a two-quart oven-safe glass bowl or baking dish with vanilla wafers.

7. Layer sliced bananas on top of wafers.

8. Pour one-third of custard over wafers and bananas.

9. Repeat layering process two more times until all wafers, bananas, and custard have been used, ending with a final layer of wafers.

THE MERINGUE

1. Whip egg whites with an electric mixer set at high speed.

2. Allow egg whites to foam, add cream of tartar, and then gradually add ¼ cup sugar a tablespoon at a time.

3. Continue whipping until sugar is well dissolved and stiff peaks have formed.

4. Add remaining vanilla and whip until well combined.

5. Spread meringue over banana pudding, making sure to spread to the edges of the dish.

6. Bake until the meringue is lightly browned, about 25 minutes.

LAURA: No, my favorite dessert is a cobbler.

DIANE: What? Not banana pudding?

LAURA: I mean, I love banana pudding. Remember whenever Grandma made it, she'd set a timer when it came out of the fridge so it could cool for a half hour before we devoured it?

DIANE: Yes, and the moment the buzzer went off, we'd rush to be the first to grab the pan, then chase each other around trying to be the first to eat it.

LAURA: That one time when I was seven, the dogs sniffed you out, hiding with the entire pudding under the dining table. I reached in with the longest-handled ladle you've ever seen and stole a bite!

DIANE: [*Laughs.*] Grandma screamed, "You're stealing dessert *from a child*!" And yet it's not your favorite?

LAURA: Second only to berry cobbler! Your favorite pie is key lime or pecan, I think?

DIANE: Oh, yes! Key lime first. Pecan second. Not far from my hometown in Mississippi is the largest pecan nursery in the world!

LAURA: Jaya's favorite is pecan pie and Ellery's is key lime.

DIANE: And you like...*cobbler*. You're sure? I find that very weird.

LAURA: Oh my Lord, and you judge my answers! Moving on: favorite book?

DIANE: *Catcher in the Rye.* You?

LAURA: *One Hundred Years of Solitude.* And your favorite flower? A gardenia, no?

DIANE: No. My second-favorite flower is a gardenia. My favorite flower, because of its spiritual significance, is the lily. I thought we had that in common.

LAURA: No, I'm not a lily person at all. Lilies are so depressing! They remind me of funerals.

DIANE: The rose represents spirituality in the West, but the lily is actually the most spiritual flower.

LAURA: But would you want it in your house? If you were going to have a bouquet to make you happy?

DIANE: I would want lilies in my house, yes. Oh, I love them.

LAURA: Do you know what my favorite is?

DIANE: No, what?

LAURA: Peonies.

DIANE: What's your favorite thing to do—besides hugging me?

LAURA: Swimming with the kids.

DIANE: Mine is dancing. When I was young, Shirley Temple was my idol. I was tapping all over the place. [*Coughing fit.*] But it's going to be a long time before I'm dancing again.

LAURA: What's the first piece of art that you remember seeing?

DIANE: My first piece of art was a diorama of flowers and rocks made by my mother. I'm going to cry. Starting when I was five, I'd watch as she dug little holes in the ground, and she would place leaves, flowers, and rocks into an arrangement and then put a piece of glass on top that she'd cover with dirt. Then you could push the dirt aside and look at the picture! Isn't that cute?

LAURA: Yes, I love dioramas.

DIANE: And then at the Catholic school, we took soap and carved a Viking boat— sticking toothpicks in the side for the oars. Oh, and Grandma would make costumes with me out of crepe paper, and we'd put a curtain up on the porch. I had these two girlfriends, sisters, and the three of us would put on shows. I pretended I was Carmen Miranda, the Chiquita Banana Girl! I took flowers out of a vase and put them on my head for a headdress. At one point my mother would play the harmonica, and we three girls would sing, "Oh, You Beautiful Doll," and we'd do a dance like we were wooden dolls.

LAURA: Genius!

DIANE: Yes, and if the audience didn't show up, we went around and got them. We'd knock on the door and say, "We've got a show going on in an hour. Bring a nickel!"

People loved the shows and would give us even more than a nickel. We started doing one every month, and it got to where we had so many people coming and tipping that we made about four dollars a show, a fortune! We'd divide it up, and it was plenty to use to go to the movies and get a milkshake. I was rich, baby!

LAURA: Where did you get the inspiration to put on your own shows like that?

DIANE: Probably from the radio. We listened to so many radio shows. My favorites were *Mr. District Attorney* and *The Shadow*! Mystery stories that always started with the sound of a squeaking door opening. What was your first memory of art?

LAURA: When I was five, I was obsessed with Édith Piaf. I made you and Grandma buy me her records, and then I became obsessed with *La Bohème*.

DIANE: No, that wasn't your first memory! Your first memory was me buying you that children's botanica book from the Metropolitan Museum of Art on Fifth Avenue. You were such a wonderful painter! You loved Monet best.

LAURA: Mom! Are you actually *correcting my memory*?

DIANE: Oh, fine. Well, I'd have said the Met books, but I guess you know best.

LAURA: Very generous of you. So, for the record, it was Édith Piaf. And then the very first movie I remember seeing was *Fantasia* at the Century Plaza Cinemas. Remember when the devil calls up all the evil spirits during *Night on Bald Mountain* by the composer Mussorgsky? I leaned forward with wide eyes, afraid to look but also afraid to look away. But in another part of the film, I laughed when the hippos, wearing tutus, danced with the crocodiles. It made me appreciate classical music better. One thing I remember about you, though, is when you loved an album, you played it incessantly for two years. On constant rotation: Glen Campbell's *Gentle on My Mind*, Herb Alpert & the Tijuana Brass's *Whipped Cream and Other Delights*, Helen Reddy—

DIANE: Oh, *I loved* her.

LAURA: Carly Simon—

DIANE: *Loved* her.

LAURA: Johnny Mathis—

DIANE: *Loved* him.

LAURA: Johnny and June Carter Cash, who were our friends.

DIANE: *Loved* them.

LAURA: But honestly, that was it. That was all the music I heard.

DIANE: I first played *La.Bohème* when you were in my tummy, and when you were growing up, I played it all the time.

LAURA: Yes, and I became obsessed with that opera. I had it memorized.

DIANE: I think you dated Jeff Goldblum because he painted that beautiful painting of *La Bohème* that we ended up with. Did you ever think of that?

LAURA: No! He didn't paint it. His sister painted it!

DIANE: Not Jeff? Are you kidding me?

LAURA: No. And I can make sure I'm right about that soon because I'm going to stay with him and his family when we film *Jurassic World Dominion*. What was the first movie you remember?

DIANE: Oh, my greatest thrill was going to the Chickasaw Village movie house on Saturdays. For a dollar or fifty cents, you could see a double feature. You'd bring your lunch and stay there all day. I saw Gene Autry and Hopalong Cassidy when I was six. A cowboy riding a horse and saving the world.

LAURA: What actors have you admired most?

DIANE: Well, Lucille Ball for one, of course.

LAURA: Me too, as you know. Didn't you meet her one time?

DIANE: Yes! I didn't tell you that story?

LAURA: I don't remember it.

DIANE: She and I were seated at the same table at the 1975 Golden Globes. It was my first big event for my first really important film role. I was up for Best Supporting Actress for *Alice Doesn't Live Here Anymore*. I was up against Karen Black for her role as Myrtle in *The Great Gatsby*. The great late actor Scott Wilson portrayed her mechanic husband, and Tom, who she's having an affair with, was played by none other than your father. Everyone thought I would win, but our movie had opened late, and many people hadn't seen it yet. When the winner was announced, it was Karen, and she wasn't there, so, can you believe it, Bruce accepted for her!

LAURA: Oh no! Dad went up and accepted the award for the actress who beat you?

DIANE: Yes. I turned to see that Lucille was watching me closely. She smiled, almost as if to say, *I've been there*. She sighed, took my hand, and drew me close to her. Then she whispered, "I was watching you when Bruce's nomination came up. I saw the look on your face, how you were pulling for him. Then just now, when you lost, he did not even give you a look because he was wrapped up in what he was going to say in front of the world as he accepted for his costar. He had an incredible opportunity in that moment to be a class act, if only he had taken some of that time to show the same compassion for you that I saw in your face for him. He could have said, 'I am accepting this award for the woman who portrayed my mistress—up against another great actress, the mother of my child!' But we women think about things like that. Most men don't. The thing is—your performance deserved to win tonight! You, Ms. Ladd, are a class act!" She smiled again sadly, patted my hand, and lifted her head away to continue watching the show.

LAURA: Wow! I love that. You know what's funny? As a kid I never saw her as radical even though that show was so ahead of its time in so many ways. I just adored her. To me, she walked on water. And she was my biggest style influence—the capri jazz pants with striped shirts and ballet flats. I feel like she should get credit for doing all that even before the sixties girls like Jean Seberg in *Breathless*.

DIANE: What did you love about her besides her clothes?

LAURA: I guess her complexity? Sometimes she's a nightmare, she's jealous, she's fierce. She walks around with cold cream on her face. When she wants to do something fun, she comes up with a zany plan. She always wants to find a way to be an actress, and she's always complaining that her husband gets to perform and she doesn't. And he still just adores her.

DIANE: You know who else played a lot of complicated parts? Barbara Stanwyck, who I ended up working with on her *Big Valley* TV series. And so did your father. He had a great arc on the show as a villain. His character even kidnapped her.

LAURA: Oh! I love Barbara Stanwyck. I remember when I was twelve that I decided she was my favorite actress. You had Simone Signoret and I had Barbara Stanwyck. I think you always liked your leading ladies a bit less slapstick.

DIANE: What did you like about her?

LAURA: For me, it was all about the banter and the irreverence, and I love dames. One of the greatest film moments of all time is in *Stella Dallas* when Stanwyck's character is standing, homeless, looking at her daughter through the glass getting married. And *The Lady Eve* is one of my very favorite movies. She plays a con artist. To get revenge on the herpetologist played by Henry Fonda, she poses as her own twin and gets him to marry her, then spends their wedding night regaling him with all the men she'd slept with. "I wonder if now would be the time to tell you about...*Herman*?" I've always wanted to find some way of remaking it.

DIANE: Oh, that's a good idea! What an amazing movie. And I told you what she did for me when you were born?

LAURA: No, what?

DIANE: After the labor I had horrible stomach pain. I learned this was from postpartum gas. A friend who'd been through this told me to ask the nurse for a tube to help get rid of the gas, easy to do. A nurse came into my hospital room. I was crying, and I asked her for the tube.

"The doctor's not here," she said. "He's busy. I don't think I can get in touch with him."

"Please, I think I'm dying!" I begged. "This is just unbelievable pain! You've got to get in touch with somebody!"

She was ignoring me while running her fingers through my flowers, which had little fake butterflies on them.

She said, "What pretty flowers! Who sent you those?"

I said, "Barbara Stanwyck."

She rolled her eyes and said, "Oh yeah, sure."

I said, "Look at the card!"

The nurse read it out loud: "Dearest Diane, I can't wait to work with you again. You are a love. Congratulations on your beautiful baby! Sincerely, Barbara Stanwyck."

The nurse stared at me with this strange look and then said, "I'll get you that tube right away." And she did.

LAURA: Ha! Did you ever tell her that story?

DIANE: I did, actually! Sometime later I had brunch with Barbara and said, "I have to tell you what you did for me. You saved my life. I was going to die if it weren't for the nurse finally agreeing to help me with my gas pain. Because of your beautiful flowers, I got my greatest gift—aside from my baby." She laughed like hell and said she was honored: "Getting someone a tube for their gas may be my crowning achievement."

LAURA: Amazing. You know, when I asked for your favorite actresses, I expected you to name two other actresses as your biggest influences. For one, I thought you'd mention Loretta Young.

DIANE: Oh yes, Loretta Young was the height of elegance and glamour. I actually thought *you* were going to say Laurette Taylor, the stage and silent film star who played Amelia Wingfield in the first production of Tom's *Glass Menagerie* and got what I believe to be the best reviews in the history of the theater. Tennessee said, "There was a radiance about her art which I can compare only to the greatest lines of poetry." She died in 1946, when I was a child in Mississippi, so I never got to see her, but I sure heard about her. The greatest of them all.

LAURA: You also talked to me a lot about Simone Signoret, who was in *Les Diaboliques* and *Room at the Top*.

DIANE: Yes, if I had to pick one, I'd say she was my favorite actress of all time, Simone Signoret. She always made me proud that I was a woman!

LAURA: OK, more food questions. What's your favorite dinner?

DIANE: Mary's chicken 'n' dumplings. Yours is my southern-Japanese casserole!

GRANDMA MARY'S
CHICKEN 'N' DUMPLINGS

Prep Time 10 mins
Cook Time 20 mins
Total Time 30 mins

INGREDIENTS

3 cups all-purpose flour

2¼ teaspoons salt

¾ teaspoon baking powder

¾ cup butter-flavored Crisco

1 egg

1 cup whole milk
(sometimes a tad more or less)

White meat of 2 fryers
(younger chickens of about 3–4 pounds)

1 can cream of chicken soup

1 teaspoon black pepper

1 tablespoon Tone's Chicken Base

1 onion, chopped

1 bell pepper, chopped

INSTRUCTIONS

THE DUMPLINGS

1. To a bowl, add flour, salt, baking powder, and Crisco. With hands or a tool, mix until it has the consistency of cornmeal.

2. Add egg and ½ cup milk, then gradually add remaining milk and whisk until well combined.

3. Using a rolling pin, roll dough out on freezer paper sprinkled with flour until it's about ¼- to ⅛-inch thick. Turn dough over, sprinkle with more flour, and roll on that side.

4. With a pizza cutter, slice into small dumplings. Put in freezer if not using right away.

THE CHICKEN

1. In an eight-quart pot, combine chicken, cream of chicken soup, black pepper (*no salt yet!*), Tone's Chicken Base, onion, bell pepper, and enough water to fill the pot three-quarters full.

2. Boil until chicken is tender, then remove chicken and set aside until cool. Remove vegetables and save for a side dish.

3. Strain liquid to leave only broth and return broth to heat.

4. Cut chicken into bite-size pieces.

5. When broth comes to a boil, add a few dumplings at a time so they don't stick together. Stir occasionally while dropping them in.

6. When all are added, reduce heat. Cover and simmer for 20 minutes.

7. Add the chicken and cook for 20 minutes more. And . . . really enjoy!

DIANE LADD'S SOUTHERN-JAPANESE CASSEROLE

INGREDIENTS

1 cup vegetable broth

1 cup water

1 cup basmati rice

Olive or peanut oil

Large handful sliced carrots

½ onion

1 turnip

1 rutabaga

1 green bell pepper

Large handful green beans, trimmed and cut into ½-inch pieces

⅓ cup tamari sauce, to taste

1½ cup broccoli florets

1½ cup cauliflower florets

¼ red cabbage, shredded

2 zucchini

½ eggplant

1 (8-ounce) package medium-firm tofu

1 small bag spinach

1 small bag shredded low-fat mozzarella

Salt to taste

Years ago, while I was in Japan promoting a film, I learned how to properly cook tofu, and to incorporate Japanese ingredients like tamari sauce, which inspired me to make a dish blending the two cultures.
—Diane

Prep Time 10 mins
Cook Time 20 mins
Total Time 30 mins

INSTRUCTIONS

1. In a pot, combine vegetable broth and 1 cup water. Add rice and cook.

2. Cover the bottom of a skillet with oil and bring to high heat. Add carrots, onions, turnip, rutabaga, green peppers, and green beans and cook until tender. Add tamari. Bring to a boil and turn down to simmer, stirring occasionally.

3. After a few minutes, add broccoli, cauliflower, red cabbage, zucchini, eggplant, tofu, and water. Cook until all vegetables are soft, stirring occasionally and adding tamari sauce to taste and water to moisten.

4. Lay spinach on top of fully cooked vegetables. Then put mozzarella on top of spinach. Cook until cheese is melted.

5. Serve over rice.

Matching suits, Malibu

Diane and Grandma Mary

✳

baby Diane

Laura, Grandma Mary, and Diane

Visiting Dad's family. Poppy MacLeish

2nd birthday

Diane and Laura, age 13

Bellina's 2nd birthday

Grandma Mary and Diane Elizabeth

7th birthday at Farrell's

Laura and stepdad Robert

with our beloved friend Scott Alsop

Diane with Shelley Winters on her birthday

Mississippi with Papa

Laura's 17th birthday

Vacation to see Paris, my dream!

en le Mediterranée

Age 14

Laura, Diane, and Mary

Diane and Laura, 1985

LAURA: That dish always makes me think of Ricardo, who we ate Japanese food with. He was such a great boyfriend to you.

DIANE: He was! His father was Japanese, and his mother was from Lima, Peru. He was a great dancer and the kind of guy who was so empathetic you almost believed he could talk to animals. He was his own person. We'd be at a party, and he never depended on me to introduce him to anybody. But he always watched out for me. If I needed a drink or something, he was there with it. I felt totally protected, and he was very intelligent and wise. Once after being charmed by a celebrity, I said, "Boy, that was really an important person, huh?" Ricardo just smiled and said, "Diane, if somebody's really important, they don't have to tell you." And yes, I guess the casserole was sort of a tribute to him.

LAURA: You made it in an electric skillet. Seventies moms were so into specialized cookware! You also had a yogurt maker, as I recall. I loved that you made the casserole with rice, tamari, and tofu, and sometimes you slipped okra and tomatoes into your black-eyed peas.

DIANE: And it's your favorite!

LAURA: Well, no, actually, sorry, my favorite food is macaroni and cheese.

DIANE: Are you sure?

LAURA: About my own favorite thing? Yes, believe it or not, I am. But I love that you keep answering these questions for me. Hey, you know how Grandma Mary would panic if there wasn't tons of food in our refrigerator? Ellery and Jaya have that. Grandma would never throw food away even if it spoiled. You'd have to really check expiration dates. You have a bit of that too.

DIANE: I know I do. I just had to clean out my fridge to move, and there were crackers, there was oatmeal, there was cereal, there was bacon, there was fruit, there was cottage cheese, there was brie, there was eggs, there was ham . . . you don't know what you're going to want at four o'clock in the morning.

LAURA: The kids feel betrayed by me if the fridge isn't full. "Mom, have you not gone to the store? There's only like three bagels and one yogurt!" Meanwhile, when I go to Reese's and open the fridge, I'm in heaven. She has these perfect rows of things—oat milks, coconut waters, just perfect. I'm so jealous. Everything is so organized. There's one head of lettuce and one perfect piece of goat cheese. I wish I cooked more.

DIANE: What are you talking about? You've been cooking through the whole pandemic! Every day you're making some new dish!

LAURA: Well, I didn't cook *until* the pandemic. I mean, I cooked a little, and I've always been a big breakfast maker. I love making those couple of pasta dishes I learned from Isabella. But I think my kids would say, before the pandemic, "Mom only cooks four things." But in lockdown, it was the three of us, and I thought, *This is my opportunity!* Ellery loves food, and so I turned to him and said, "If we could make any food in the world, what would it be?" And that kicked us off into this odyssey of trying new recipes all the time: jambalaya, East Indian curry, Cajun shrimp. It was such a bonding activity, gathering in the kitchen with the kids and watching YouTube cooking videos, teaching ourselves how to make things we wanted to eat. We even took some lessons with Courteney. She's become a great cook.

DIANE: Ellery got really into hibachi recipes, right?

INGREDIENTS

2 eggs

4 boneless skinless chicken breasts, cubed
in bite-size squares

1 head of broccoli, chopped

3 carrots, chopped

Dash of smoked paprika

A few sprigs of fresh dill

3 cloves of garlic

Dash of garlic powder

1 tablespoon ginger paste

1 lemon

2 cups long- or short-grain white rice

1 teaspoon flaked sea salt

1 tablespoon ginger, minced

Dash of onion powder

Black pepper to taste

1 tablespoon ponzu sauce

1 tablespoon rice vinegar

4 filets of fresh salmon

1 tablespoon soy sauce

2 tablespoons teriyaki sauce

1 yellow onion, finely chopped

1 zucchini

2 tablespoons grapeseed oil (divided)

ELLERY'S HIBACHI

Prep Time 10 mins
Cook Time 20 mins
Total Time 30 mins
Serves 4–6

INSTRUCTIONS

1. Preheat oven to 365°F.

2. Cook rice in rice cooker.

3. Chop all veggies into squares or quarters.

4. Marinate the salmon. You can start this as early as the night before with rice vinegar, teriyaki, soy sauce, lemon, garlic powder, and 1 tablespoon of grapeseed oil. You can also put dill on top.

5. Bake the salmon for about 15–18 minutes, reserving the marinade.

6. Remove dill from marinade and discard. Add ginger and garlic. Sauté chicken in the mixture for about ten minutes until cooked through.

7. Simultaneously, in a large pot (you will add all ingredients to this) sauté garlic on medium-low heat with the remaining tablespoon of grapeseed oil.

8. Add all veggies, sauce ingredients, and cooked chicken.

9. In a small bowl, scramble eggs, then mix into the pot. Make sure they are thoroughly cooked.

10. Mix the rice in with the mixture once eggs are cooked.

11. Serve with salmon on top.

LAURA: Yes, and I created a master list of movies to watch with the kids, including recommendations from you, Dad, Steven Spielberg, and David Lynch. We've already gone through two-thirds of it.

DIANE: Oh, what are everyone's favorites so far?

LAURA: *Being There, The Wizard of Oz, The Godfather* and *The Godfather Part II, Defending Your Life, The Lady Eve, Rear Window.*

DIANE: Oh, you know who I talked to yesterday? Aunt Johni B.

LAURA: Everyone's favorite relative! She is the greatest. Ninety-five years old and she still sends the kids presents every year. Every time she leaves a room she says, "First one who talks about me is a son of a bitch!"

DIANE: Every. Single. Time.

LAURA: So we did a lot today. Are you ready to go now?

DIANE: Yes. Hey, should we make chicken 'n' dumplings with the kids tonight?

LAURA: Sure! That's a fun idea. Wait here and I'll go get the car.

DIANE: Sounds good. Hey, Laura, come back!

LAURA: What is it, Mom? Are you OK?

DIANE: First one who talks about me is a son of a bitch!

LAURA: [*Laughs.*] Good one.

A FAMILY MOVIE LIST AND A FEW INSPIRING ACTRESS HEROES
(CLOCKWISE, FROM TOP LEFT: SIMONE SIGNORET, BARBARA STANWYCK,
LUCILLE BALL, JEANNE MOREAU, LAURETTE TAYLOR, LORETTA YOUNG, AND BETTE DAVIS)

DIANE'S AND LAURA'S BEDSIDE TABLES

Laura

It's hilarious to me how my mother wants us to have the same favorite things. This is one of those areas in which as parents what we say and what we do can be pretty different. Looking around my home and hers, I see some ways in which I'm a lot like her and others in which we are very different.

My mother loves nothing more than to hang art around her house. She has pictures from all the movies she's done. I have exactly one movie poster: Alexander Payne gave me an incredible Italian poster of *The Wild Angels*.

I do love movie memorabilia. I have a shelf of cool stuff, like Shelley's suitcases and my blaster from *Star Wars: The Last Jedi*. And I do decorate with the same basic ideas my mother and her friends always had: that nothing should ever feel uncomfortable to anyone who comes to your house and that your children should be able to romp through the place without being yelled at. Mom always believed that the things you have should tell a story—a chair your grandmother gave you here, a caftan from Anthony Quinn there.

I'm still nowhere near as nostalgic as my mother about old movie sets. I don't have hundreds of mementos on my wall. Will I when I'm eighty? Maybe. For the first time, at fifty, I've just hung up a photograph of me on a set: David Lynch gave me one of him, me, and Kyle MacLachlan on the set of *Blue Velvet*. It's in my hall, and when I pass it, I think happily of those friendships, and I think, *Maybe this is why my mom has all those pictures up*.

But the fact is, I only have to look at our bedside tables to see how very different we are. My mom's bedside table has tissue boxes and medicines and spiritual books: *Jonathan Livingston Seagull* and *Secret Places of the Lion*, esoteric astrology. Mine is, midcentury marble and holds Bach flower remedies, Rescue Remedy for sleep, books by Gabriel García Márquez, and feminist literature like bell hooks. I like considering these differences because they help me see the ways in which I'm my mother's daughter and where I'm my own woman.

"That one time when I was seven, the dogs sniffed you out, hiding with the entire pudding under the dining table. I reached in with the longest-handled ladle you've ever seen and stole a bite!"

—LAURA

DIANE AND BRUCE, CHRISTMAS, EARLY SIXTIES

WALK

11

DATING, DIVORCE, & DINER MENUS

DIANE: What a pretty day. Can I sit down on this bench?

LAURA: How about we walk a little first? [*Breathing in deeply.*] Ah, feel that sun on your chest!

DIANE: The sun feels good, but it's hot today, baby. Look how pretty the ocean is. I may not want to be in it, but I want to be near it. As long as I don't see any fins.

LAURA: Nothing's going to bother you. If a shark comes, just shoo it away.

DIANE: Shoo it? Like the nursery rhyme? "Shoo fly, / Don't bother me." Sure, that'll work.

LAURA: Didn't you used to sing a song called "Shoo-Fly Pie and Apple Pan Daddy"? Or did I make that up?

DIANE: No, you're not making that up. It's actually "Shoo-Fly Pie and Apple Pan *Dowdy*." A pandowdy is a kind of pie. When you dowdy a crust, you cut into it while it's baking. "Makes your eyes light up, / Your tummy say 'Howdy.'" Dinah Shore sang it.

LAURA: Oh, wow. Okay, Mom, in all our conversations, there's been one question that I realized I've wanted to know my whole life.

DIANE: Well, you better ask it, I guess. 'Cause, honey, if I'm dead, you can't ask me, right? So we should do it now.

LAURA: Yeah. And I think it's something that all kids of divorce like to hear from their parents.

DIANE: You want to know if your daddy's really your daddy.

LAURA: [*Laughs.*] Yeah, I look exactly like him, but you never know, right?

DIANE: You laugh, but I had my DNA done, and my cousin's, just to prove that we weren't being lied to.

LAURA: Wow.

DIANE: Did you know I did that?

LAURA: No. I think my shocked face doesn't lie.

DIANE: I sure as hell did. You're never too old for curiosity. We didn't uncover any secrets, though. And yes, your father is definitely your father, a hundred percent.

LAURA: Okay, good. I'm glad we resolved that. I mean, we look exactly alike, but you never know.

DIANE: Okay. So what was it you wanted to ask?

LAURA: Well, I've asked you what went wrong with Dad, about your dynamic and why it didn't work. I guess children of divorce, maybe we never ask, as though we don't want to bring up old wounds to a couple who are no longer together. But I never have asked you much about what you loved—not only about Dad, but about your marriage, what you were like together. You told me about the first time you slept together, which I can never unhear. I get the infatuation and attraction. But I'd love to know more about the later parts, also—after I was born, how it was for you. I mean, I don't think I'm the first child of divorce to look at her parents and think, *Huh. I came from that. What was it like? When I was running around oblivious as a small child, what was going on in my parents' world?* Maybe for years after a heartbreak you don't want to talk about the good stuff, but I realize now, when I talk about Ben and me with our kids, that they have a hunger for those sweet stories. I want them to know they came from a love story. I want them to know what worked, what was great about our connection and our marriage, and what I admire about their dad. Not only his talent, but things that are deeply personal. And I'm just wondering if you'd like to do that with me.

BRUCE AND DIANE, MRS. MUNCK

DIANE: You want the truths today, with a capital *T*!

LAURA: I do.

DIANE: OK. Your father is a great, great actor. That's why I worked with him even after we divorced, when I directed him in *Mrs. Munck* in the nineties.

LAURA: I know you respect him as an actor, that you admired him for breaking away from his family. But you've also shared so much about what didn't work. Today I'm interested only in what did work.

DIANE: Well, I— *[Coughing attack.]*

LAURA: And then I killed her.

DIANE: *[Laughing hard.]*

LAURA: I just think all kids, at any age, like to imagine their parents happily in love when they were little. Could you share for me what it was like?

DIANE: Sometimes I think maybe we avoid the deep feelings we felt in a relationship because we don't want to miss it. You know, it almost feels like fate, you asking me this today. I had dinner last night at an Indian restaurant, and these two people behind me were talking. The man, who was probably about sixty, was crying about his relationship with his mother—he was not over it. And the woman was competing with him. She said, "Well, I had it *really* rough, as a child of the Depression." I looked over and laughed. That woman never went through the Depression! She was nowhere near old enough. You see how we cling to the negative and hold on to the past wounds and play that tiniest violin for the saddest song to ourselves.

LAURA: Oh, let me be clear, Mom: I'm not trying to—

DIANE: No, I meant me. I'm saying you're right that I have at times been too quick to see the bad parts of my marriage to your father and to ignore all the good. So you want some positives. OK. First of all, what I loved with your father was the laughter. Laughter feels like love. Laughter is so healing, as long as it's not at somebody else's expense. And his laughter was not at somebody else's expense. He wasn't somebody who tore other people down to make himself feel good. He has a brilliant mind. You know he has a photographic memory.

LAURA: Yes, he can recall the name of every kid I played with in kindergarten. Bellina and I are always blown away by how much he remembers from our childhood.

DIANE: I know. It's incredible. What was great about our marriage was the communication. It wasn't competitive, even though we were two actors. We understood each other's work, and there was compassion there. Only some other actor couples had that—maybe Joanne Woodward and Paul Newman or Eli Wallach and Annie Jackson. They were all friends of mine.

LAURA: What would you guys do for fun?

DIANE: Besides acting? We worked a lot. Our work was our fun. But I suppose we'd play cards or Monopoly with friends. We'd take walks, swim. We loved to go to new places, drive around, see sights, check out new places to eat. He could cook a little bit, your dad. He was not a great cook, not like my dad, but he was a good cook.

LAURA: He was? I don't think I've ever seen him in a kitchen.

DIANE: Well, maybe I'm making that up. That's pretty funny. We do trick ourselves. But maybe he just appreciated my cooking so well that I imagined him in the kitchen doing it himself.

LAURA: Would you go to the theater together?

DIANE: Yes, we did. We'd have a wonderful time discussing plays, talking about performances.

LAURA: It must have been nice to share that passion for acting and to be able to discuss it all the time.

DIANE: That's right. We would talk deeply about acting.

LAURA: Ben and I had that, too—talking about music and film, sharing the love of art. So great.

DIANE: Yeah, that's beautiful. Where our paths divided was when it came to questions about life, questions like *Why are we here on Earth? To do what with our soul?* I would say that our body is just like a car for our soul to drive around in, and your father would make jokes about it. He'd say, "My body I see. How do I know there's a soul?" He was not someone who would ever—

LAURA: *[Laughs.]* Oh boy, here it comes.

DIANE: Well, I'm sorry, but he took this soul for granted. I know I'm a little woo-woo, but I'm very interested in spiritual evolution. I'm a "high intuitive," highly sensitive to other people's energy. People talk about the sixth sense, but I'm interested in the seventh. As an actress I can entertain you. But if you don't like it and my performance makes you sick, I have some healing gifts and I can cure you. And if that doesn't work, I'm also an ordained minister, so by God I can bury you. So I'm a really good friend to have! When the amazing Shirley MacLaine was out on a limb, I was already out on the branch!

LAURA: Well, I'm lucky to have you as the seeker and Dad as the irreverent one. Maybe you balanced each other?

DIANE: Well, yeah, I was the seeker and your dad was being sought...by other women! Oh, boy, now I'm getting into betrayal. It's hard to stay on track.

LAURA: Look, I'll never fault you for any negatives. He's your ex-husband. These are feelings you deserve to have. But it's also a joy to hear positive memories of you and Dad. I want to hear about a night at the movies or a night of card playing with friends or something silly he did.

DIANE: OK, one time we played Monopoly with his agent and his agent's wife. The men got mad and threw the pieces everywhere. We women just shook our heads.

LAURA: I can't believe I never asked these questions before. I wonder why I waited so long.

DIANE: I don't know, Laura. Kids don't want their parents to get divorced.

LAURA: It's just funny—when I looked back at our walks, I realized, "Wow, I've never asked my mom, 'Is there still love there?' or 'What did you love about him?'"

DIANE: No, I'm sorry, I am not still in love with your father.

LAURA: Well, I know *that*.

DIANE: But I always loved your father. *I* can say anything bad about my ex-husband, but nobody else better say anything bad about him!

LAURA: And what did you love? That is the very specific question that I'm interested in. Right now I have that you could talk about acting with him and he made you laugh.

DIANE: Well...the sex.

LAURA: I'm going to vomit.

DIANE: It got you here, didn't it?

LAURA: Well, it's just so specific.

DIANE: Sorry. It's the truth. He was a very thoughtful lover and could be very romantic.

LAURA: You've told me he would leave notes on the pillow, right?

DIANE: Yeah. The bad thing, though, was that your father had lied so much as a child. His parents didn't do anything about it. He just preferred stories that sounded good, even if they weren't true. If a true story wasn't good enough, he liked to make it better.

LAURA: Ha, I know. Every time I repeat a story he's shared, I realize it sounds a little too good, and I have to wonder if it's true or an exaggeration.

DIANE: Yes, most of them are probably not true. And yet he's had a fascinating life, and so some of the most ridiculous, unbelievable ones might be completely accurate. He appreciated a cozy home and he had good taste. He let me do pretty much whatever I wanted to in terms of decorating. He was very easy to please that way, because I have good taste, I think. We enjoyed making a home together. And whatever I wanted to spend, he didn't care. As long as we had a dime, he didn't care if I spent it.

LAURA: That's sweet. Well, you don't have to keep going. This is more than I've ever gotten. I like thinking of you decorating your home and laughing and playing cards. Thank you.

DIANE: I'm so glad you're asking these questions. Most people won't until someone's gone. Now your turn. What about a fun memory of you and Ben from when the kids were young?

LAURA: Well, Mom, you knew us as a couple. You were around for all my stuff. That's why *I'm* trying to get stories out of *you*.

DIANE: Indulge me.

LAURA: Oh, OK. Well, I was thinking about one time when you and Ben and I were at 101 Coffee Shop with the kids. There was a catfish sandwich on the menu. Do you remember this?

DIANE: Oh, ha, I think I do.

LAURA: We were looking at the menus when Ellery started crying out of nowhere. We were startled, and we all looked at him and asked him to tell us what was wrong. He turned to you and said, "I don't want to eat *caaaaaat!*" It took a minute, but we realized that he'd seen the catfish sandwich on the menu and freaked out. And the three of us had to reassure him that there were no cats being served.

DIANE: Oh, I remember that. [*Laughs.*]

LAURA: Ben and I locked eyes and tried very hard to suppress laughter as you said to Ellery, "No! It's just a fish that *looks* like a cat!" Which sounded adorable, so he cried *more*. Ben and I were covering our faces, trying to hide how much we were giggling. But you said, "No! It's hideous looking! Strange! A fish with whiskers!" Which was also somehow not very reassuring. Anyway, eventually we got Ellery calmed down, and it was a very sweet moment. Ben and I laughed about that for a long time afterward.

DIANE: What else?

LAURA: Ben loves this story, and the kid love hearing it. Remember when I went into labor with Ellery? Ben and I had decided to have a home birth.

DIANE: I was against it.

LAURA: Yes, you were. One of Ben's favorite memories that we laugh about still and the kids love is how you had emphasized your concerns about a home birth over and over again. But we were prepared and we were firm about it. We were only a few minutes from the hospital. This was how we wanted to do it. Fully in labor, I begged Ben for some crushed ice. You'd come over to check on me. You were standing together in the kitchen getting the ice and you said to Ben, "You know, Ben, one of the reasons people have babies in hospitals is because hospitals, unlike homes, are clean and sanitized." Ben was explaining that in fact there was research proving that there's a lot of bacteria in hospitals. You argued that on the maternity ward everything was sterile—in any case far cleaner than our house. You said we should consider taking me there right away. Ben said, "Diane, this house is *spotless*. We've prepared. Everything is under control and perfectly sanitary." At that moment, our dog Buddy walked between the two of you and vomited *everywhere*. You just looked him in the eye and said, sweetly, "I'll clean it up."

DIANE: That dog had the best timing.

LAURA: Ha. Buddy did have your back with that one.

DIANE: So now that it's been a few years since the divorce, how's dating going? You're not seeing anyone, are you?

LAURA: Well, I haven't mentioned him to you yet, but I have had a few dates with someone. But because of our schedules and work we haven't been able to see each other much. He's brilliant, he's hilarious, and he's so wonderful to be with. But he's going through his own life dramas. I wish I was able to see him more, and sometimes I feel weird that he's not more available, even though I'm busy too. I mean, after a great night, if I don't get a call or a text, I still get my feelings hurt and feel vulnerable.

DIANE: Ab-so-lutely.

LAURA: When I didn't hear from him after the last time we saw each other, I assumed it was over. Then a girlfriend of mine went to a dinner party. While she's there, she's talking to a guy, and she says, "Oh yes, I met you with my friend Laura Dern!" And he says, "Oh my God, she's so cool!" And my friend says, "You should ask her out!" And he replies, "I couldn't do that! I'm friends with the guy she's dating."

DIANE: Oh no!

LAURA: When she told me this, *I thought, I haven't even told my BFF that I had a fling with this person and now here's his friend describing us as dating?* If we are, he forgot to tell me! Aren't you supposed to check in with someone to tell them you're dating?

DIANE: Darling, you got involved with this man who's too busy, for whatever reason, to even communicate, and yet he's scaring off other people? Laura, there's really something wrong with that picture! If it's this bad when you're dating, what do you think would happen if you ever married him? You might not see him for a year, and he says, "Oh, say hello to my wife for me when you see her."

LAURA: *[Laughs.]* Yeah, well, I've been hurt so much in the past that I think I prefer to avoid complicated relationships rather than risk dealing with trust issues again. I mean, I think in my twenties and thirties, I wasted so much energy trying to be everything to someone. I'd say, "I know how I'll change this person! I'm going to be the person who's going to help open him up and prove my worth!" I think I wore that ability as a badge of honor or something, but it's not my job. I think when you're strategizing all the time like that, you end up in a relationship with someone where you can't go deep, you know? I think it's really difficult even in the best situations to really let go and trust someone fully. Do you still get jealous?

DIANE: Oh, sure. My mother was jealous with damn good reason. I think because of her influence I've often been jealous without any reason at all. Recently, I picked up Robert's phone because it was beeping. A woman had texted him something that seemed flirtatious: "Why haven't I heard from you? I always feel so good when I hear from you!" *Who the hell is this?* I wondered. *How dare she?* Instantly this red flush ran through me. Before I could even stop myself, common sense just flew out the window and I texted her back: "Thank you for being so considerate and kind to *my husband* and making him feel good. That's so delightful of you. Signed, The Wife." She texted me back: "Oh, I've always wanted to meet you, Diane. I've told Robert what a fan I am of yours. You know, even though we're cousins, we haven't seen each other in ages!"

LAURA: Ha! Serves you right!

DIANE: Well, she took my sarcasm for friendliness, thank goodness. Still, I was *mortified*. Robert fell off his chair laughing when I told him about it, but I think he was kind of pleased that I was jealous. When I lecture, I tell women, "You say, 'He cheated on me! He did this to me!' He didn't do it to you, baby. He did it to himself! And he will pay his own karma. Every piece of pie is paid for sooner or later. No one really gets away with anything." Do you get jealous?

LAURA: No more than anyone else—or maybe a lot more. I'm not sure, frankly. It's depended on the man and how safe I've felt. But I've had boyfriends who made me miserable, suspecting me of cheating. They'd say, "I saw you flirting with that waiter!" Meanwhile, they were cheating on me!

DIANE: Who would you say is the love of your life?

LAURA: Mom! I can't possibly answer that question. Sometimes I listen to you sharing about the loves of your life and I've got to say, another thing you've given me is the opportunity to really cherish all the various forms love has taken in my life. By listening to your stories about the different loves of your life, you're helping me to understand that there doesn't have to be just one designated soul mate. That's been my experience thus far. It wouldn't be fair to say there's one. I've had a few great loves, and I've been able to learn from them and grow. But I could never name a love of my life. Because I feel like I'm at midlife, and who knows what's to come? Ask me again in twenty years. When you're one hundred, I'll tell you who the love of my life was.

DIANE: I'll hold you to that. The way you're walking me these days, I feel like I might get there.

LAURA: But you know who I thought was going to be the love of my life when I was twelve?

DIANE: Ha! I think I do. Tell me the story.

LAURA: It was when I did *Foxes*. Jodie Foster was the female lead, and the male lead was—

DIANE: Scott Baio!

LAURA: Yes, and at the time he was eighteen, and the hottest guy in America. You and his family kept trying to make a plan to get together, and finally you settled on New Year's Eve. To me this meant: *He wants to spend New Year's Eve with me! That means he wants to kiss me at midnight!* I dressed to the nines in my new satin Hang Ten jeans with a matching satin jacket. Both were in ice blue, a color that you told me matched my eyes. My eyes were very evident, you'll recall, because I wore Coke-bottle glasses—with frames I believe also in ice blue. Very seductive.

DIANE: Oh, please, you were adorable!

LAURA: So they arrive: Scott, his parents, and . . . a ridiculously beautiful, very adult-seeming teen girl model. I was hoping she was a cousin. Scott looked incredible in his white leisure suit. This was the *Saturday Night Fever* era, after all. We walked into your very 1980 all-white living room with the overstuffed couch and the shag rug and the glass coffee table. It felt like Scott and I were swimming together through a cloud. And then my fluffy little dog walked in. And of course, because he's perfect, he loves dogs.

DIANE: Naturally.

LAURA: "Oh my God, I love dogs!" he says. "What's your dog's name?" This is where I think the humiliation began, because this is when I said, "Christmas." He said, "Oh, cute! Why?" Me: "Because I got her for . . . Christmas." This was me showing him my very inventive mind. And then, in our cloud-filled moment, we looked in each other's eyes while he cuddled my puppy, and I thought, *This is it. He only sees me. He likes me. I know it.* Then I saw his face change. He was looking down. I followed his glance and that's when I saw it: Christmas had gotten her first period all over his white pants. I didn't even know dogs got periods, or even really what periods were, exactly. But I knew enough to be very, very upset.

DIANE: Oh!

LAURA: And this is not the end of the story! Mom, you do remember you brought me club soda, cheerfully saying, "Soda water will get it out!" And I knelt before this potential love of my life, trying to wipe the blood out of his pants. Even worse, Mom, and this should be a public service announcement, *soda water does not get blood out of a white leisure suit*. If anything, it sort of spread the blood around so there were pink patches.

DIANE: [*Laughs.*]

LAURA: But it's OK. He was very sweet about it. And the night ended beautifully... with me eating a Milano cookie from Pepperidge Farm while watching him make out with the teen girl, who was in fact his girlfriend. The sweetest thing? You came over to me and gave me a kiss on the cheek and stole a cookie from my plate. At least I had my mom. You even brought me a glass of milk.

DIANE: They *are* the best cookies to dip.

LAURA: I was so clueless about boys. In general, I feel like in this country we don't tell girls enough about sex. Even though you may be one of the most progressive moms I know about sexuality, you never talked to me about orgasm or any of that stuff.

DIANE: That's not true! Remember when you were eight and we went on that cruise with Erica Jong?

LAURA: Yes, it was an artists' collective cruise of writers and actors! Richard Dreyfuss stands out in my mind as especially hilarious company.

DIANE: I bet you overheard a lot.

LAURA: I did. I actually got a lot of confusing information. Erica Jong's lecture was all about the female orgasm, but it was completely opaque to me. Then after the lecture she had a book signing and I grabbed a copy, opening to a drawing that I still haven't figured out. The picture, which I can see clearly to this day, was of two people cross-legged on their backs with their knees touching, having sex. It looked very comfortable but very gymnastic at the same time. To this day, I don't really understand how that works.

DIANE: [*Laughs.*] Could I get that book? Maybe someday I'll try that out for us and tell you how it was!

LAURA: I wish in retrospect that we'd actually discussed that stuff in a real way. It might have saved me some time sorting it all out later.

DIANE: Hmm. Maybe I wasn't being inclusive of the big picture, or in truth maybe I was too embarrassed or too shy. That's my generation! I put a scene in my film *Mrs. Munck* where she says, "When I was a little girl my mother was so hell-bent on modesty, to ensure it, when I took a bath, she put blue dye in the water so that I wouldn't see my own privates!" That scene was actually based on an experience a friend of mine had as a young girl.

LAURA: Well, you certainly never sheltered me. When I got to RADA in London as a teenager, I unpacked my suitcase and found you'd sent me with about a million condoms. But then you seemed shocked when I lost my virginity.

DIANE: Well, I didn't give you condoms so you'd *use* them.

LAURA: Next time let me know that the cases of condoms are purely *hypothetical*. You know, in so many films—comedies, dramas, television, in the zeitgeist—it is a common shared experience that we don't want boys to feel shame. It's known that when they come into their sexuality, you don't want to embarrass them. I had this conversation with Cheryl Strayed and we talked about how it is so amazing that for boys sexuality is a given and for girls it's still so taboo.

DIANE: You're right. And of course for girls the risks around sex are greater. I remember once when you at thirteen came home from school and said, "Mom, do you know a lot of the kids in my class have already had sex?" My God, you were only a freshman in high school! Inside me was this giant scream that I did not let out! Instead I forced myself to take a breath, keep my composure, and gently ask, "Well, Laura, and how do you feel about that?" You replied with one of the wisest statements I've ever heard. My own child said, "Well, Mom, you know, I don't think they realize even though their bodies might be ready for sex, emotionally they are not ready." That's the truth of the heart. I was flabbergasted. I thought, *If only we could teach the children that if you respect yourself, if you're going to share your body, you have to really be ready*. Remember when I asked your dad to have a conversation with you and Bellina about sex?

LAURA: I know you like to tell this story.

DIANE: Yes, I do. I said, "Bruce, you have to help me. I'm a single parent here! I can't do this alone! It's your daughter and her best friend, whose mother is also raising her alone and wants help with this! They're turning twelve! Sex is talked about on TV all the time. I need some help here with these girls to guide them properly, protect 'em now they're going to be teenagers soon! I'm desperate!" He said, "OK, don't worry.

I'll take care of it." And then he takes you and Bellina out for ice cream and you're in the back seat, still with little glasses, pigtails. You tell me later Bruce says, "I want to talk to you girls, OK?" You're both like, "Uh, OK." And he says, "Uh, I want to talk to you about *sex*." And you're both, "About sex? Uh, OK." Right?

LAURA: Well, that's not exactly how I remember it, actually.

DIANE: He said, "The worst thing that can happen to you is that, before you're ready, you could get knocked up!" And you girls said, "Knocked up?" He just goes on and says, "Make sure the guy always wears a raincoat." You were both super confused about why a man would need to wear a raincoat during sex. And to make it all worse, in a *Playboy* magazine interview he proudly told the story of how he helped his daughter and her friend stay safe by making sure they knew all they needed to know! I almost killed him.

LAURA: I actually have to admit, Mom, I think Bellina and I were laughing really hard. Dad's irreverence has been probably the trait I most appreciate in and share with him.

DIANE: It's true. Your father is hilarious. But I just assumed it was traumatic for you girls.

LAURA: Well, I could have done without him sharing the story in *Playboy*, but...maybe I felt relieved since I'd lost my virginity the year before.

DIANE: What?! What the hell are you talking about? Laura!

LAURA: And...that's the irreverence I was talking about. I'm bullshitting you.

DIANE: You're supposed to be trying to save me! You're going to give me a heart attack.

LAURA: I did think he was being funny. Though you are right that I was confused for years about why a man would wear a raincoat during sex.

Laura

I do get my irreverence from my father, but my mom and grandma certainly passed along many incredible traits of their own. One that I've been thinking about lately is a strong belief in all manner of superstitions. It makes me laugh because I still stick to most of them with great commitment.

Like so many other families, we have phobias that have been passed down through the generations and affect the way we go about our lives. For example, my dad will freak out if he so much as sees a snake on TV. He turned down a role in *Gandhi* because he was afraid to be in proximity to a snake in a scene. This fear has spread to the rest of the family. One time we were in Lake Tahoe and Ellery discovered a snake in the house. He caught it with tongs and ran it outside to set it free. While passing through the rest of us, we all screamed like we were characters in one of Tennessee Williams's plays. FYI, the snake was *tiny*.

I personally am freaked out by spiders. (The one exception being *Miss Spider*, an animated children's show I'd watch with the kids when they were little.) I think the root of my arachnophobia is the time I was bitten by a black widow spider at six years old, an incident which forever altered my eyesight. So to this day they aren't my faves.

Grandma Mary was scared of elevators and would always take the stairs if she could. But my mom is the one who is a completely fascinating dichotomy. She is the most fearless rule breaker, activist, and artist you will ever meet and yet, as a parent... or when it comes to the existence of the great white shark (no help from master Steven Spielberg), she can be overwhelmed by terror.

One way our family combatted our fears was through superstitions. They don't have the spiritual significance or the gravitas of a family legend. But they hold the idea that this is just what we have to do so things don't go wrong. My grandma had all kinds of rules for everyday living. My mom inherited some of her obsessions, though she denounced a lot as well. But for the ones that did stick, she perhaps expanded upon them and then gave them to me. And now I have passed on quite a few to my own children. As a result, we can't walk on either side of a pole without breaking the curse by shouting "bread and butter." This will protect us from ever being separated, of course. Obviously, one should be concerned when a black cat crosses their path, and make sure they never walk under a ladder. And, I beg you, don't step on a crack, you'll break your mother's back! I suppose I should apologize at this point because there is a chance I've just now passed the superstitions on to you. But, while I'm at it . . . Never go outside with wet hair, you might get the flu. Oh, and if your nails are wet from a manicure, stay away from an open flame—you might blow up. *You're welcome.*

What none of us talk about, those of us who keep these traditions alive, is that the underlying messaging is: if everything's going wrong, what tradition did you forget that made this happen? Or perhaps only those of us who take rules so seriously think this way . . .

Recently, my family had just had dinner and the kids wanted to go swimming. Jaya was leaping toward the pool when Ellery said, "Jaya, we have to wait thirty minutes!"

Jaya replied, "Why do we have to wait thirty minutes?"

He said, "You could get a cramp after you eat. You have to wait!"

They both looked at me with a sense of mistrust and Jaya said, "Ellery, look that up. Where did you hear that from?"

"Well, Nana told Mom, and Nana's mom told Nana."

Suddenly they both realized that the idea did not seem right. So, we got on the internet and learned that the idea that you can cramp if you swim right after eating is a total myth. The article traced the myth back to public pool owners who didn't want children throwing up after they ate, so they started a rumor that many have adopted as truth. (I have no idea if this origin story is true, but I've already been believing a myth my whole life.)

It's amazing to think that I and generations before me have waited at least a half hour after any meal in order to swim. And there is nothing anatomically that can make it hard for you to swim after eating! So many hours of delayed joy. I was very grateful to Jaya and Ellery for freeing themselves and future generations of this nonsense.

But of course, you should still NEVER step on a crack. Please for god's sake.

Our family rules...

don't step on a crack..
       (you'll break your mothers' back)
don't ever put a hat on a bed..
don't swim after you eat..
        (you'll get a cramp)
don't walk under a ladder..
don't sing before breakfast..
       (you'll cry before night)
don't cross a black cats path..
don't let a pole come between you
(if you do, you must both say)
      "bread and butter"
   to break The Curse?

if you get served with two forks,
     you'll be invited to a wedding

if your ears burn,
    someone is talking about you.

if you spill salt,
   throw it over your left shoulder
    to stop bad luck.

always say say see you later ~
    never say goodbye

LAURA AND MARY WITH DIANE ON HER WEDDING DAY TO ROBERT

WALK

12

FISH IN
FLOWERPOTS

LAURA: On our last walk, I pushed you to talk about the happy things in your marriage when I was a kid, but I feel like I should let you open up about some of the bad ones too. Divorce is so hard. We've both been through it now. And I wonder if now, as one divorced woman to another, and maybe without judgment or shame directed at ourselves or other people, we can talk about heartbreak.

DIANE: OK, where should we start?

LAURA: Maybe when I was little? Mom, I realize that as a kid I heard more than I should have. To be honest, it was only about two topics: money and infidelity. That was all I ever heard.

DIANE: Oh. I thought we hid that from you. When we got divorced, you were only two, after all.

LAURA: Yes, but I was around for the years of fallout. You kept fighting after your divorce, and I couldn't help overhearing it, whether it was about child support or a tuition payment. You'd bring up old resentments, and it would get into "How could you say that? You're the one that cheated!" They were muffled fights that weren't always all that muffled. It was painful. And I say it now with no judgment, because I know despite all the therapy, all the wisdom, I know there were things that I allowed my own kids to hear when I was triggered or angry.

DIANE: Well, I'm sorry that you heard that, but it's true that he *was* the one who cheated. And it was hard to talk to him about money.

LAURA: You know a photo that I think about all the time? The one where Dad is pushing me on that fire truck he gave me.

DIANE: Oh, you loved that thing! It had a bell, and you rang it over and over.

LAURA: Yes, that's true. In the photo you can see that my dad is proudly walking me down the street with my favorite Christmas present. I loved being with my dad. I loved that present so much. I might not have seen Dad as often as I would have liked, but I was so happy whenever he was with me. I only felt it as a special moment. But to me, that photo is a perfect example of how we choose to see only the good in images of the past, not the full story, which in this case is that for the two of you the sadness around the divorce was still raw and you guys were miserable. And yet I think you worked overtime to give me a loving home filled with playdates and fun.

DIANE: I'm realizing that we've still never talked much about your divorce. I've never asked you before: Were you unfaithful in your marriage?

LAURA: No, I never cheated. Never ever.

DIANE: I never cheated on your father. I don't remember cheating on any man in my life.

LAURA: I cheated on somebody once.

DIANE: OK, maybe I did too one time. *Maybe.* I'm sure I haven't been perfect. Jesus said, "Don't throw the first stone!"

DAD, GRANDMA MARY, AND ME

LAURA: I was with someone who I later learned was not free and clear, but I was told by him that he was free and clear!

DIANE: Oh, please. You're not responsible for that.

LAURA: No, I had a responsibility to another woman, and I failed her.

DIANE: You didn't know!

LAURA: Yeah, but you know, it's still shitty. And if we really want to know the truth, and we're really looking, we can see it. I probably just didn't want to see it. I wanted to believe the story that sounded most like a fairy tale.

DIANE: You know the story about my father's mother, Grandmother Hattie, and his father, J. J., cheating, right?

LAURA: No.

DIANE: They were living in Mississippi, and Hattie was pregnant with their first child. A neighbor called her on the phone and said, "Your husband's running around on you. He's meeting up with another woman tonight!" And the neighbor told her where! Well, Grandmother Hattie grabbed a shotgun and went out in a horse-led wagon. Soon she came across his horse and a strange horse tied up to a fence along the road, beside some woods. She ties up the wagon and starts walking toward some breathing and gasping that she hears, just a little way off. Granddad was on a blanket with the woman, in the middle of going at it. He was interrupted suddenly by the light of a flashlight on his face and the click of a safety catch being released on the gun. Then he hears the voice of his wife say, "Finish!" He says, "What in—?" She said, "You heard me! Finish!" Then she said, "Now, mister, get up and zip up your fly! You started something else you're gonna by God finish! You started a marriage and father-hood and you're gonna by God finish that! And miss, that's my man." She patted her gun and continued, "I'm a spiritual woman, but if I ever catch you with him again, it's in me to just blow your head off, set it on a stump, and walk away saying prayers! Now, Husband, c'mon!" She tied his horse to their wagon and drove home. On the way, he tried to talk to her, but she wasn't having it. When they got home, she refused to discuss it. She just sat down at the piano and played until she went to bed. The thing is, she never brought it up again! Didn't hold it over his head or make a big deal about it after that night. I don't know any other woman like that! And if Granddad J. J. ever cheated again, Grandma Hattie sure as hell never found out! They went on to have fourteen children together.

LAURA: Wow—fourteen kids. Is that a happy ending? Mom, if you'd only told this story on your first dates, no one would have ever cheated on you.

DIANE: [*Laughs.*] In 1992 I appeared on a talk show on the Lifetime channel called *Attitudes*. Two of my fellow guests that day were Susan Faludi and Gloria Steinem. Boy, it was a hot talk show. I talked about how upset I was made by some of the scripts I'd read and the sexist attitudes of so many executives I'd encountered. I shared a quote from the great Martha Mitchell, wife of Nixon's attorney general: "When women stop competing against each other like dogs after a bone, then and only then will we truly be liberated." The whole audience went crazy cheering! Then I added to it: "No woman could ever catch her husband in bed with another woman if there wasn't another woman there doing it with him!" And with that the crowd got a little quieter.

LAURA: Yeah, no one wants to own their own role in these things. I've been guilty too. One time I spent the whole night with an ex-boyfriend crying over our breakup. I never slept with him, but my boyfriend at the time acted like it was a betrayal any-way. Maybe it was.

DIANE: Well, kid, that isn't cheating.

LAURA: But it felt like cheating to him! It can be awfully hard to forgive that sense of betrayal. But you also don't want to be totally unreasonable. This is something so many of my friends have dealt with: Do we blame ourselves because somebody doesn't know how to deal with animal instincts, or gets drunk, and you throw away a long marriage because of one night? Do you save a marriage if he cheats fifteen times? You have to look at what your boundaries are.

DIANE: You've had some rough breakups. The one when you were engaged to—

LAURA: Mom, I'm going to stop you right there, because I don't want to hear his name and because I can't believe you're going to repeat this rumor. That's someone that I never would have gotten engaged or married to and somehow you're believing the tabloids. And every time I read an article about myself, people say I was engaged to that person. The same way people always say I had some supersexy affair with John Cusack, whom I've never even kissed. I cannot believe you are saying the engagement thing now. In spite of all the articles out there that say we were engaged, no, we were never engaged! I was engaged at twenty-three to Jeff Goldblum, very briefly. But I was too young to make that commitment, and we both realized it. I'm very blessed to now call him a friend, and I adore him and his wife and his little boys. But that's it for engagements in my life except the one that became a marriage with two beautiful children.

DIANE: Well, why does everyone think you were engaged to him?

LAURA: I guess because he married someone else while I was off making a movie and that didn't seem dramatic enough for people, so it had to include a broken engagement too?

DIANE: I guess it was bad enough.

LAURA: Yes, and to get over it I went on a road trip with my amazing friend Jamie around the country, and we took a bunch of photos where I was flinging my arms out to the sides as if to say, "I surrender! This is me starting from scratch! Life starts over now!"

DIANE: And once again, you're in a new phase now, one I know something about.

LAURA: That's right. I'm a fifty-year-old woman who's had my kids. I would love to find a partnership at some point that is really committed and really sexy and really vital, a partner with whom I could travel the world. But I don't know that I need a marriage ever again! Relationships for me could be way more liberated and liberating now that I don't need any specific label from a man. I don't need them to give me babies. I don't need them to be my husband. I certainly don't need them to raise my children. I've done those things. So now I can have intimacy purely because I want to have connection. Not because I'm looking for someone to have a family with. I already have my kids. It feels less daunting. Freer. Sexier.

DIANE: You deserve it. Well, I can't wait to meet the next man you fall for.

LAURA: I'll consider introducing you, but you don't have the best track record on that.

DIANE: What are you talking about?

LAURA: One of my first proper dates, when I was a junior in high school. A really cute boy asked me out. We came back after dinner, and I was so excited for you to meet him. I came down the hall with him and opened the door and you were sitting in front of the TV watching *The Ten Commandments*, eating little ice cream bonbons. At the moment I opened the door, you had a bonbon in one hand and were biting your other fist. You screamed, "Oh God, no! The lions are eating the Christians!"

DIANE: Oh yes, I remember! That boy was *cute*. What happened with him?

LAURA: I think you scared him off because he never asked me out again.

DIANE: Well, I promise to do better next time. I'm so happy to hear you're open to dating now and that you have such a positive outlook. It took me a long time after my divorces to feel that way. They really threw me for a loop, and after each of them I made some poor choices. You know, after your father and I broke up, I never should have married so quickly the second time. It was 1969, and I was in a bad place. I was in that Off-Broadway play *One Night Stands of a Noisy Passenger* with Bob DeNiro.

LAURA: I don't think I've heard of that show!

DIANE: We were struck during previews—stopped from opening—and it was a real shock. There I was in New York, no money, away from my child. You were being taken care of by Grandma Mary in LA. I was depressed. And along came this really great, handsome guy—William Shea Jr. He looked like Jack Lemmon. We were both newly divorced and looking for love!

LAURA: How did you meet him? I never asked.

DIANE: Connie DeNave took me to a Mets game and introduced me to Bill there in the box, whispering to me as she did that he'd also just gotten divorced. I didn't know that she'd already told him all about me and that our meeting was planned. Nevertheless, he was so vulnerable himself that he'd invited two other girls to join him—protecting himself! They were all over him, flirting, carrying on. One of the reasons why, which Miss Naive here didn't know, was that the whole damn stadium was named after his father! Seems he was kind of smitten with me, and he said, "Let's go

DIANE IN ONE NIGHT STANDS OF A NOISY PASSENGER

have a drink," I said, "OK." We went out on a date that night and then went back to my house and we started kissing. Boy, could he kiss! He was a real southern smoocher. Those southern boys always kiss with a lot of passion, a lot of gentleness. He said, "Diane, now look, I know you just got divorced, and I wouldn't want to lead you on. I wouldn't want to sleep with you and have you fall in love with me. I'm not ready to get married again." Well, that statement pissed me off! I mean, really just bugged me so bad. I was challenged. I said, "Oh really? You want to protect me? You're afraid that if I slept with you that my heart might float away? You know what—don't worry about that." I kissed him and curled his toes. And then two weeks later he got down on a knee and proposed.

LAURA: Two weeks? He asked and you said yes immediately?

DIANE: Yes, immediately. It was like a scene out of *Alice Doesn't Live Here Anymore*. He got down on one knee, holding a beautiful ring, right in the middle of the restaurant! It was so romantic. I was lonely, and my play was closing, and I said, "OK!" And then I thought later, *What have I done?* I didn't know him well. The next day I called him and said I had to go back to LA to be alone for a while and get some clarity. He ran after me within twenty-four hours! Shelley said, "Go talk to my therapist. You are running from real love. You have a man—a gentleman—who comes from a great family, and he's gorgeous, and he'll take care of you, and he loves your child."

LAURA: What are you talking about? He hadn't even met me.

DIANE: Right, maybe it was, "He would be a good father to your child." I said, "Oh, Shelley, stop it." She said, "You're going to my therapist, and I'm going to pay for it." And she took me to her therapist. I told him all my reservations. He told me that I was wrong and Shelley was right! He agreed I should marry this man!

LAURA: Then two years later you called the therapist and said . . .

DIANE: "I was right and you were wrong! Quit your job!"

LAURA: You didn't do that.

DIANE: No.

LAURA: I wish you had.

DIANE: Me too! OK, so Bill was lonely too. He was a lovely man in so many ways. He never should have been a Wall Street broker. He was a great composer.

LAURA: I liked his two sons, and I liked it when we were all together sometimes as a family, but I'm sorry, I had a really hard time with Bill.

DIANE: Laura, you were five. The truth is, kids don't ever want their mothers to date.

LAURA: No. I liked many of your boyfriends. But Bill had all these weird rules, like if there was one pea left on my plate, I'd be in trouble.

DIANE: I never saw him do that. I can't abide people who make others eat when they don't want to! Laura, are you imagining this? I got furious at my friend's husband for doing that to their daughter!

LAURA: I know!

DIANE: That's a terrible thing to do! I don't know how you remember much of him at all. When you came there to New York to meet him, you were five years old. We all went on a honeymoon together to Florida. Remember that?

LAURA: I do.

DIANE: With the boys and you and Mary, and, oh my God, his ex-wife was nearby staying with her family, who had a home in Florida. That's part of why my honeymoon was in Florida in the first place—so she could see the boys!

LAURA: Mom, anybody who goes on a honeymoon with all the kids, and brings her mother to take care of the kids, and picks the spot so the ex-wife can visit? It was very considerate of you, but that marriage doesn't seem like it's made to last.

DIANE: Well, that one certainly wasn't. He and I lasted less than two years.

LAURA: I just had a flashback to when, right in the middle of the chaos of that divorce, you got recognized on the bus. Do you remember?

DIANE: I think so. I was on that soap for a while, originally called *The Storm Within*. Then they got a sponsor: Ex-Lax. "*The Storm Within*, brought to you by Ex-Lax!" That wouldn't work. So they changed the title to *The Secret Storm*. I played a poor girl named Kitty Styles. I was a replacement for the original actress, so I was actually Kitty Styles Number Two, but I had a big following. Girls would flock to me saying, "Oh my God, it's Kitty Styles!"

LAURA: Right, so when you were going through your second divorce, we had to move from the apartment we loved in New York that we only lived in for a couple years. And so ended our brief stay on the East Coast. I went back to LA and that was that.

DIANE: Oh, did you love that apartment too?

LAURA: I loved being a child living in New York—riding Big Wheels with Bellina down Fifth Avenue, skipping through Central Park, wandering through museums. It was so magical. How old was I?

DIANE: We lived there when you were five, six, and seven. You went to Park Avenue Christian Day School.

LAURA: Yes, and we went to museums, the opera. You took Bellina and me to *Aida* and *La Bohème*. At home we would blast *Free to Be . . . You and Me*. I was taking ballet. And Drew and Scotty were very sweet stepbrothers. It was nice to have them around. You converted the office into an indoor jungle gym that I climbed all the time. I was obsessed with it. And we played on the roof, looking out over the city. And I was obsessed with the PBS show *Zoom*. One day Ben Stiller came to a show of Ben's and stopped short when he saw Ben's percussionist, our buddy Leon. He said, "Oh my God, you're Leon Mobley from *Zoom*!" *Zoom* had been a big deal for Ben in the seventies too.

DIANE: But you were saying something about the divorce.

LAURA: Divorce is never a blast. But I will say that was a particularly miserable time for all of us, as I recall. And we'd been away and had to come back to New York to pack everything up. And while we were gone one of my fish had gotten pregnant and had babies. We'd had four fish when we left and now there were dozens. You and I bagged up all the fish—

DIANE: I do remember this! We didn't have bags—we put them in flowerpots!

LAURA: That's right! And we took all those fish with us onto the city bus.

DIANE: Why didn't I just spend the money on a cab?

LAURA: I had two pots. You had another. And we rode all the way downtown from Ninety-Fifth and Fifth, with the water sloshing around!

BIG WHEELS AND MY PUPPY, CENTRAL PARK, THE NEW YORK YEARS

DIANE: Yes—to that good pet store that took great care of all their pets. We couldn't take care of them ourselves, but we didn't want somebody feeding our precious baby fish to a piranha!

LAURA: There we were on the bus. I was seven, holding pots and scared the fish would jump out. And then this woman came up, and she said, "Kitty Styles!" I thought to myself, *Oh my God, please do not talk to my mom right now. We are on a very important mission and in a whole lot of ways this is not a great time.*

DIANE: That was a dark period in our lives.

LAURA: It's such a relief, Mom, to hear you talk about how overwhelmed you felt. The truth is, no matter what kind of divorce you're getting, you feel like this life commitment you've made is falling apart at the seams. It's such a lonely feeling, even if you're divorcing someone who's a coparent or who you have a valued friendship with. I don't remember what you looked like in those moments with Dad. I was two. That's why I have so many questions for you about what it felt like. Unfortunately, I'm asking them now, not six years ago when I felt like I was the only person on the planet who'd ever gotten a divorce. Every day was like living inside Pedro Almodóvar's *Women on the Verge of a Nervous Breakdown.* But I mostly hid it, as I think women often do. Even my closest friends who'd gone through divorces had hidden away at their most broken moments. But you saw my most broken moment. Do you remember?

DIANE: What are you talking about? All I remember is you working so hard to take care of the kids. You seemed very strong and together through all of it.

LAURA: No, Mom. Think back to the night you came over when I knew the family home was about to be dissolved and we'd have to move sooner than I'd thought. And the holidays were coming. I was going to break my kids' hearts. And I had to find a home quick and get a tree and create some sense of family tradition. You came over to advise me on how to do it. And first you started talking about money, which stressed me out. Then you referenced your second marriage, which we both have triggers about. And then you started telling me what I shouldn't be doing that I was doing. I can't remember what your advice was. It may have been excellent. But I started to tell you to stop telling me what to do . . . and that's when I blacked out. I'd been sitting on our seven-foot-long, very heavy couch. The next thing I knew, I was holding the couch over my head. And yes, I threw it. I didn't throw a lamp or a small chair. I threw a seven-foot couch while screaming, "You have no idea what I'm feeling right now!" Of course, you did have some idea. You'd been divorced twice and were on your third marriage. But at that moment I felt completely alone in what I was dealing with. Do you remember your reaction?

DIANE: [*Laughs.*] Honestly, no. Did I yell at you? I hope not.

LAURA: Mom, have you really blocked this out? It was only six years ago. No, quiet as a church mouse, you walked into the kitchen and said, calmly, "I'll make us tea." And then you turned in the doorway, looked at me, and added, "Don't forget, Laura, you have scoliosis." Meaning I shouldn't be picking up heavy things.

DIANE: Ha! I'd forgotten about that. Well, I might have been worried for your back, but I am quite sure I didn't blame you for throwing furniture. Divorce can make anyone crazy.

Diane

When you first fall in love with someone, you want to tell each other everything. And when you meet a stranger on a plane, you think you're never going to see that person again, and so you feel free to tell that person everything. But a relationship that lasts many years is something else. Emotions are very powerful. In a fight between emotions and logic, emotions win every time. And often you wind up cutting off both. The feelings are so powerful that you can't handle them, and so you pull away. It happens between parents and children and between husbands and wives. There are moments where you failed the other person by covering up something or telling a lie. Parents cover up all the time because we want our children to love and respect us. We aren't shrinks. We don't have a degree on the wall. We make it up as we go along. You're scared. And so you shade the truth. You want your child to do what you want your child to do. You want to maintain your authority. You want the child to respect you. I think there was a time when I lied and Laura realized it and yet was not in a position to confront me. And there are ways in which Laura has surprised me, not been completely honest. We are all unknowable, ultimately. On crime shows, the killer's mother says "My child would never do that!" But you don't know. On these walks, Laura wants to speak and hear the full truth. I'm pretty sure something's going to get said eventually that will hurt me. It's my job to try to take it gracefully. That's the parent's job, isn't it? I know there are things Laura could attack me for. And there are times she's wounded me too. What is worth bringing up? What will it help to talk about and what will hurt too much?

"There we were on the bus. I was seven, holding pots and scared the fish would jump out. And then this woman came up, and she said, 'Kitty Styles!' I thought to myself, *Oh my God, please do not talk to my mom right now. We are on a very important mission and in a whole lot of ways this is not a great time.*"

—LAURA

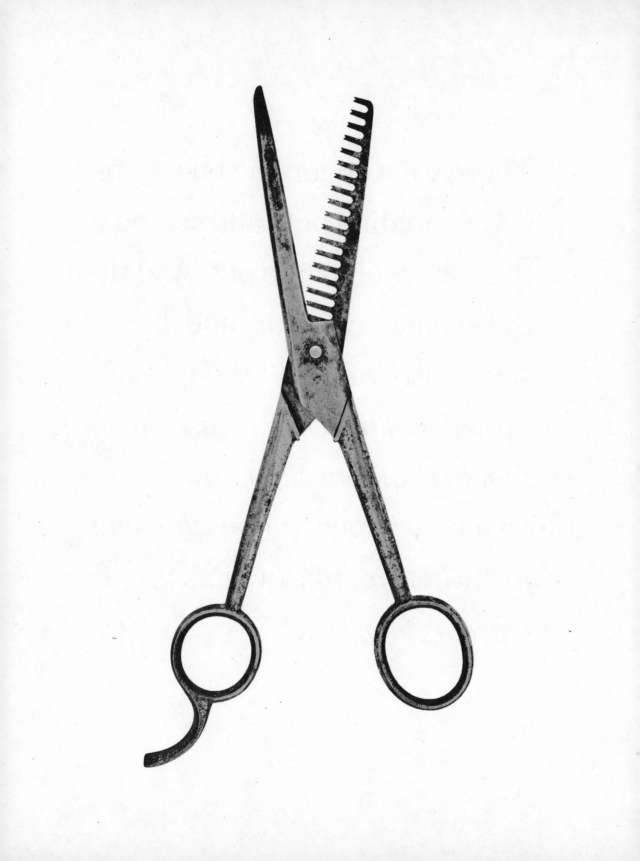

WALK

13

THE HAIRCUT

DIANE: I feel great today! Let's walk a mile! My lungs are finally healing.

LAURA: Thank God.

DIANE: New tissue is being formed. And the scar tissue is going away. It's amazing, unbelievable.

LAURA: You know, one thing that I think could be interesting to talk about today is being mothers and being working mothers—the gift but also the stigma of that.

DIANE: The stigma of it?

LAURA: Yeah.

DIANE: What does that mean?

LAURA: The stigma, for women, of trying to be mothers while also working. That's something that your generation shifted so dramatically for so many women. When you were young, most people thought women couldn't do both.

DIANE: Oh, I did both, but I never did really understand how I did it, or how anyone does.

LAURA: You know, I don't think I've ever thanked you for setting a such good example for me as a single mom. When I think back on the beginning of my divorce, the pain of splitting, the horror of telling the kids, the longing for it to be civil, and the prayer for coparenting or a friendship—I didn't reach out to you. I didn't ask those questions about how it might go. In that first stage I was so afraid of the idea of the kids not having their dad living in their primary home, the way I hadn't. But I will say that of all the things I was afraid of for them, I didn't feel terror about being a single woman raising kids. Truly because of how strong you were in the face of it yourself.

DIANE: I don't think any daughter ever gave her mother a better compliment than that. That's lovely, Laura. Thanks.

LAURA: Yes, in all things, you've always said to me, "I'm going to do this! How? Who knows? But I'm going to figure it out!" I'm carrying so much anxiety right now. I'm still feeling a lot of pressure even right now. School stuff. Track team. Trying to get a job. Paying the bills. I don't know how I'm going to juggle all of this.

DIANE: Oh, honey! It's fine! Let's just walk to the next bench and breathe.

LAURA: Ha, you're telling me to breathe now! Look at how the tables have turned.

DIANE: Oh, sweetie.

LAURA: I feel like my daughter needs me. And frankly I need her. We're lucky that now women in the workplace receive some accommodations. It's a fight, but sometimes we have the luxury of being able to have our babies with us on set.

DIANE: Back in my day, you could never have a child on set. You hear these stories about Lucille Ball helping implement day care at Desilu, but these were not conversations on the kind of independent movies I was doing. It was really hard, especially if you weren't the boss and if it wasn't being financed around you.

LAURA: Remember, even sometimes when you were the boss it was hard! Think of Martha, our director on *Rambling Rose*. She was told to please not nurse her baby around anyone.

DIANE: They made her put a blanket over her head while she was nursing her child!

LAURA: And they asked her never to do it on set because they said the crew would consider her weak.

DIANE: Oh God. That's right—unbelievable, isn't it? But it happened!

LAURA: A woman being able to feed a human being is a sign of weakness! It's infuriating!

DIANE: But a bunch of us complained and said we wanted her to feel safe on our set. Over time, those kinds of moments have really led to a change, but we had to fight for it.

LAURA: One day in season one of *Big Little Lies* I so wanted to bring Jaya to set. She was ten and she didn't have school and wanted to be with her mom. There was this little voice in the back of my head: *It's a workplace. You want to seem professional. Maybe having a child around would be distracting.* But I fought that voice because I know my kid and she is incredibly respectful of what I need to get done. I knew she could even help me run lines and be my assistant for the day.

DIANE: You were like that! A joy to have around wherever I took you.

LAURA: That's sweet. Well, the minute Jaya and I got there, Reese said, "Oh, fantastic! Jaya's here! My daughter can hang with her! And the boys were planning to go play basketball at the court nearby, so they can all go." And then Nicole Kidman walked in and said, "Oh, great, my girls wanted to see Jaya!" I realized that we had effectively created a *Big Little Lies* day care.

DIANE: Brilliant!

LAURA: That speaks to Reese's and Nicole's leadership as producers. Also, the whole show is about motherhood! We found a way to create a community where we as women were supporting each other in our families' needs as well as our work's needs. From then on, the kids were there anytime they wanted to be. And I believe that rather than hurting the show, having it be a family-friendly set helped it. We were better at our jobs knowing that our kids were safe and happy and welcome.

DIANE: It is so much better now, certainly.

LAURA: And yet, even though it's better now, it's still so hard sometimes. I wanted to talk to you about it because you had Grandma. And Grandma and you, separate from your mother-daughter relationship, were incredible partners in coparenting me after you and Dad divorced. I was so grateful for it. And she was amazing.

DIANE: Absolutely.

LAURA: Of course there's such a difference between the mother-daughter relationship and the daughter-grandmother relationship. Your connection to Jaya is so different than your connection to me.

DIANE: Of course it's different. You feel less worried you're going to damage the child, and you have less responsibility, and you're at a place in your life where you're older and wiser. And you have less fear for your grandchildren than you do with your own children.

LAURA: And you've said that you've had your own resentments of your mother, as we all have those to work out with our parents.

DIANE: Everybody does.

LAURA: You have a right to resent your own mother, and I have a right to feel only tenderness and sweetness toward her. I mean, she got a lot of the fun stuff with me because you were away working. It wasn't until I saw that same hurt on my own children's faces when I wasn't there because I was working that I really understood you. I can only hope they come to understand it one of these days.

DIANE: They will, honey. They will. And you'll apologize to them the same way I am to you now, and what a gift you'll get if they receive your apology in the same spirit as you. Listen, there are a whole lot of women who did not work outside the home and poured everything into mothering and still bungled the job. It's also possible to be great at both work and home. But absolutely, that pain is real.

LAURA: The most extraordinary and kindest parenting guide I've ever known was a woman named Mary Hartzell, who created the magical preschool the kids went to. I was sharing with Mary that I knew what it felt like to miss my actress mom and I didn't want to put my kids through that. And she very generously looked at me with her face filled with so much love and said, "I don't know, Laura. Maybe they chose a vagabond creative life. Have you ever thought about that?"

DIANE: That's lovely!

LAURA: Of course then the principal of another of the kids' schools said, when the kids were little, "You know, it's hard for these kids because their father's life is so inconsistent. The life of a musician! They don't know when he's home and when he's touring. That must be so hard on you, but at least they have the consistency of their mother being there every night giving them dinner, giving them their baths." And I said, "Uh, no. My schedule's weird too. I'm an actress." And her face dropped. I saw a woman crushed with worry for my children. It was traumatic! And she didn't hit Ben with any of that, only me!

DIANE: That's terrible! Laura, I'll tell you something. You were lucky. You learned more by being with me than other kids who had stable households. You've got to go backstage, meet politicians, see people from all walks of life. You saw a lot more than others. You got an education, girl. And you got some wisdom from those lessons.

LAURA: *I got to meet politicians!* Is that meant to be a *highlight*?

DIANE: [*Laughs.*]

LAURA: Look, Mom, you keep defending working motherhood. I'm not saying it's wrong. Obviously, I'm doing it. Most women have to do it. I'm just saying that it's not always easy. I was talking about my kids' principal giving me a hard time about my parenting, and you immediately jumped in to tell me that I had an awesome childhood and learned so much from all the adventures you gave me.

DIANE: I'm not defending it! I'm stating a fact! You've learned a lot from the life you've had. You've evolved.

LAURA: But once again I'm trying to be honest with you about some real pain, and you're coming back at me with, "Sounds like you don't appreciate the amazing life you had!"

DIANE: Well, I did trust Mary completely.

LAURA: Yeah, at least you knew I was safe with her.

DIANE: And that's worth every penny, kid.

LAURA: And I knew that about our sitters.

DIANE: Yeah, that's right. And when I wasn't working and I came to pitch in, you could trust me, too. I did my best to do things right for you and Ben and the kids.

LAURA: Oh, I just had such a traumatic memory.

DIANE: What? What is it?

LAURA: [*Groans.*] I'm really glad you'd pitch in, but—

DIANE: Oh my gosh, what is it? I see a moan at the edge of your lips. What are you going to tell me?

LAURA: It's just what you said—you'd pitch in and get things done the way you thought was right.

DIANE: That's all a grandparent can do.

LAURA: What about when you cut Ellery's hair?

DIANE: Oh, my God! I can't believe you're bringing that up. One time when you and Ben were gone out of town, and I was playing Grandma, Ellery said to me, "I want to get my hair cut." I set it in motion and then you were so mad at me.

LAURA: Robert told him he should get a haircut. It didn't start with Ellery; it started with you guys.

DIANE: No, no. I didn't even.

LAURA: Yes, you did.

DIANE: No.

LAURA: Yes, Robert told him his hair made him look like a girl.

DIANE: Well, it *did*.

LAURA: Gross, Mom.

DIANE: Was I even married to Robert then?

LAURA: Yes, Mother.

DIANE: Are you sure?

LAURA: Yeah, you were married to Robert before I met Ben.

DIANE: Oh, that's right, I've been married to Robert for twenty-three years, and Ellery's twenty. Hello. And he was six at the time. So . . . Laura, this was fourteen years ago! And you still sound mad about it!

LAURA: There is no statute of limitations here. You led the witness, one hundred percent. You made Ellery embarrassed.

DIANE: Oh, please!

LAURA: Thinking that boys can't have long hair is just so outdated, Mom. It really smacks of homophobia and gender bias. We should be raising our kids with a sense of freedom and openness toward their own self-expression.

DIANE: Woo-boy! No, Laura. He *asked* for the haircut.

LAURA: You are such an actress! That is not true! And it was wrong. Would you want someone to tell you how you should look or what little girls or little boys "should" dress like or be like? Come on, it's the twenty-first century! Your generation was rigid around gender identity, but his generation is so much more progressive, and—

DIANE: Have you ever stopped to think maybe you wanted a little girl at that time? And that's why you kept his hair so long?

LAURA: Oh. My. God. I cannot believe you just said that.

DIANE: Listen, he could have said, "I like my hair. I don't want to cut it." But he wanted his hair cut, Laura. And I said, "Oh, you want to go to the haircut place with the balloons?" He said, "Yes." I said, "Well, let's do it." And I took the child and got his hair cut. God almighty, you and Ben went crazy, like I'd gotten him a tattoo.

LAURA: Crazy? He was our baby! I'd like to get him a tattoo right now: "Don't listen to your grandmother."

DIANE: He was almost six! That's old enough to decide that he wanted a haircut.

LAURA: He had the most gorgeous hair! And you convinced him to be embarrassed of it. And I don't for a second believe that he asked for that haircut.

DIANE: He did, Laura! On my breath—and I don't have that much left—he did, Laura!

LAURA: No way.

DIANE: That day I left your house in a huff, went and parked the car, and sobbed my guts out. That was wrong of you.

LAURA: I feel completely right about that, actually. I'm still livid. I'm getting angrier by the minute.

DIANE: You treated Grandmother wrong. You did. I would never have treated my mother that way if she'd cut your hair. And she did cut your hair! Many times! I didn't always love the haircuts, but so what? I loved her. She did plenty of things that I didn't agree with, but I never sent her away sobbing.

LAURA: Yeah, well, you have to get over that. I was devastated. It wasn't just the haircut; it was that you said he looked like a girl and also that he shouldn't paint his toenails, which I *loved*. But you told him it was girly.

DIANE: I didn't tell him he looked like a girl. I said it to you, but never to the child. Never.

LAURA: Then Robert did.

DIANE: Well, hell, he's from Texas. What can I tell you?

LAURA: I know. But guess what? We're trying to raise a new generation of open-minded kids who don't have this stigma that says, "Boys don't cry. Girls need to speak only when spoken to."

DIANE: We agree on that. All of our evolution is two steps forward, and one step back. And the step back's really rough.

LAURA: "Cross your legs, be a lady." Whenever people said that, you'd say, "No way. I'll speak when I'm ready to speak."

DIANE: I've always said, "*Lady* is a four-letter word."

LAURA: But how hard is it on boys to hear the message that they're not supposed to feel free to be emotional? And for women to hear that they're not supposed to have their own voice?

DIANE: Never! I never said that! I'm an actor! I want grown men to cry! You know, I don't think we're ever going to be on the same page about the haircut. I believe that it was not just about the haircut, ultimately. Laura, hair for a man is a symbol of power—

LAURA: Oh, it was definitely about the haircut. You're totally full of it right now.

DIANE: Wow. Fourteen years later, it's still raw.

LAURA: For the record, I feel completely right about what I felt that day.

DIANE: Good for you. Thump your chest like Tarzan. He said to me: "I want my hair cut."

LAURA: You are a liar.

DIANE: Don't you dare call me a liar.

LAURA: Archaic conservative thinking!

DIANE: Please. Your liberal denial is—

LAURA: Oh, Mom. Do not bring politics into this.

DIANE: You said "conservative"!

LAURA: Ben and I were devastated.

DIANE: *[Sighing.]* I'd like to go home now.

LAURA: Good. Me too.

Diane

The haircut! Fourteen years ago, and Laura's still holding it over me. I guess that's the kind of thing that can never be put to rest. The only thing you can ever get to is for me to say, "I think it was out of hand for you to be rude to your mother." And she can say, "You used us being away to do what you wanted to do with our child. You were wrong."

I still think *they* were wrong. Ben and Laura thought he looked cute. I'd taken him for haircuts before, but just for a trim. "Two inches!" they'd say. But then they were out of town! And yes, there was a meaning to my method. But I did not spur him on. He really said to me he'd like to have his hair cut. So we did it. He looked great. They gave him a balloon. He was so happy. Then Laura and Ben came home, and Laura went frigging nuts. It felt rude to the poor old grandmother.

I left in a huff, and I went to my car and parked on the side of the road and felt sorry for myself and sobbed that my daughter could talk to me like that. I never wanted to see them again. I never wanted to set foot on their doorstep again. It became a mountain, not a molehill. They apologized later, but the damage had been done. Not a good thing. I was heartbroken. Laura got me on the phone and told me to come back that night. I can't remember if I did or not. It was so painful. I took that photo out of the scrapbook of my mind.

Did Ellery want it cut, or did he just know I wanted him to want it cut? It's fourteen years too late to figure that out, but it's still bothering both of us. Those things never leave your consciousness. You try to get over it, and so many loving, tender things take place in between the flare-ups, and all you can do is hash it out and know where you stand and agree to disagree.

This conversation may seem like a failure, but it's not. When you have old conflicts that go undiscussed, it's like riding an elevator that's rattling and that makes you feel unsafe. You don't know when it might just crash to the ground. These conversations, even if they're tough, make those ropes stronger. They help you ride up and down in life with less fear of a sudden drop.

"When you have old conflicts that go undiscussed, it's like riding an elevator that's rattling and that makes you feel unsafe. You don't know when it might just crash to the ground. These conversations, even if they're tough, make those ropes stronger."

—DIANE

ADELAIDE DRIVE

WALK

14

OUR
OLD STREET

LAURA: Hey, I'm sorry the haircut came up yesterday, but I'm also glad. It meant a lot to me that you called last night to clear the air. It feels like there's nothing we can't talk about if we can talk about our old fights.

DIANE: It's true.

LAURA: The weather feels like a London day. So cloudy, and there's a chill in the air. You know what that makes me think of? That time we stayed in London at some apartment near the Thames. It was when you were dating Al.

DIANE: I remember that trip. One night when we were out to dinner with Shelley, Omar Sharif came to the table. I had such a crush on him.

LAURA: After *Lawrence of Arabia* and *Doctor Zhivago*, who didn't?

DIANE: Shelley said, "Oh, Omar. I want you to meet my friend, a great actress." And he kissed my hand and said, "Oh, Diane Ladd. I'm such a fan of yours."

LAURA: Al was there for that?

DIANE: Yes, you and he were both sitting next to me. You kicked my foot when he kissed my hand. I think you were scandalized. Meanwhile, all I could think was, *Boy, I wish Al wasn't here.* I was trying to break up with him. He was a cheater. He was a great man in his own way, but—

LAURA: No, he wasn't.

DIANE: Well, maybe not. He was certainly holding on to his problems. CEO of a big company. Good-looking guy. Could be quite a gentleman. But it turns out he wasn't such a good guy.

LAURA: Certainly not.

DIANE: You know, I was thinking this morning as I waited for you that it's very hard to see the truth, or to see the sun when it's hidden behind a cloud. And you help me try to remove the cloud, to let the sun shine on us. That's all we can do. We've learned something from this ourselves, and I just want to tell you, I thank you for choosing me as a mom. And I love you with all my heart.

LAURA: That's lovely, Mom. Thank you. I love you with all my heart too.

DIANE: And thank you for helping me fight for my life and prove that doctors, like anybody else, can be darn wrong.

LAURA: Amen.

DIANE: And boy, have I had fun lately. I sure am glad I stuck around.

LAURA: I am sure glad too. Now you need to keep taking care of yourself. And given how strong you've become, I think we should go this way today.

DIANE: The sun is coming out from behind the clouds, but it's still cold. Wait, why are we on this block?

LAURA: Mom, I don't want to freak you out, but I really think we need to do something hard today. You're strong enough.

DIANE: Laura, actually, can we go home now? I'm getting cold. It's freezing. My throat is clogging up.

LAURA: Why don't you put your shawl over your shoulders? Here, I'll help you. And then let's walk this way today.

DIANE: Adelaide Drive?

LAURA: Yes, Adelaide. Mom, this is our old street, huh?

DIANE: Yes. Oh my God. It looks the same. Ooh, but, honey, it is cold here. Maybe we should do this another day.

LAURA: No, let's go see the old house. It's just down this way. Come on. Mom, I couldn't sleep last night. I was thinking it might be healthy for us to finally talk about the thing we haven't talked about all these years. Also, I haven't come and looked at this house in who knows how long, and I bet you haven't either. So please do this with me. Is this the house?

DIANE: Oh, look at that runner go! Oops, let's step out of his way so he doesn't have to break his stride.

LAURA: Hey, Mom, is this the house?

DIANE: No. Wow, it's really windy on this street, isn't it? I'm thinking I should go back to the car and pick up one more layer.

LAURA: The sun is fully out now, Mom.

DIANE: The sun is high, but it's still just too windy!

LAURA: Is this the house?

DIANE: No.

LAURA: *This* is it! Right?

DIANE: Yes, Laura. This is the one. That's where your father and I got divorced.

LAURA: And where I was born! No need for the divorce to be the main memory. Divorce as a memory trumps even the birth of a child? Jeez!

DIANE: My God. It is a pretty house. The view here is like a peep inside heaven, isn't it?

LAURA: Yes, how gorgeous is that?

DIANE: Before I got divorced, I really should've said, "Hey, Husband, before you run off and leave me, you have to at least buy us this house." It was only *150,000 dollars!* It's worth millions today!

LAURA: Millions? Wow. But regrets don't serve us, right?

DIANE: It's cold. Let's leave.

LAURA: Just a little while longer.

DIANE: I've got to be careful. I can't get pneumonia again. That was the last thing the doctor told me.

LAURA: You won't get pneumonia standing here five more minutes. We'll just look at the front of the house and smell the jasmine.

DIANE: I'm going to be in the hospital cussing you.

LAURA: Well, let's not do that. Let's just look at this house a bit. It's incredible.

DIANE: Greta Garbo lived here before we did, you know.

LAURA: No!

DIANE: Yes. So did Peter Lorre. Your dad and I used to laugh about it: whose vibes each of us picked up, Lorre or Garbo? This living room had a stairway up to a loft that I used for a writing room, way up there in the back.

LAURA: It's a Craftsman, right?

DIANE: Yeah. I should have just bought that house and stayed right there.

LAURA: You brought me home to this house?

DIANE: I played in the yard with you out there. We were starting over with you. It was a blessing because your father and I had been through so much, Laura. We didn't have therapy or grief counseling back then. We could barely pay the rent and we were struggling. Everything was difficult. This was the house we moved to when we finally were able to get away from our previous home where we went through everything.

LAURA: I don't think I've heard you say her name in a long time.

DIANE: Diane Elizabeth. I don't know how everyone talked me into naming her Diane. Generally I don't like naming a child after a parent. I named you Laura because I wanted you to have your own unique identity, but I gave you Elizabeth so you and your sister would share a middle name. You were our new joy. I've held all this grief in. It's hard to get it out, but I can't believe we've never really talked about it.

LAURA: I can only imagine how hard it's been.

DIANE: My girl, you are the blessing of my life. I owe it to you to talk to you about it. When one child dies and another child is born, I think it's hard on that child in so many ways. I was bound and determined to protect you. On the other hand, I was bound and determined to teach you to protect yourself. I'm sure I got the balance wrong.

LAURA: Are you saying you were both overprotective and underprotective? Like your Richter scale may have been off? I think that might be true, and my God, completely understandable. I'm sure it's why I never did drugs or anything too insanely reckless. I didn't want to give you more to worry about. I am so sorry, Mom, for you and Dad. What immeasurable trauma. Almost from birth, I could feel that something devastating and heartbreaking had happened. Do you want to share more about that time?

DIANE: It hurt physically, like it does now that I'm sick—sharp like a stab in the heart. Time burnishes the edges, but the pain never goes away. One moment you feel good inside, you trust God that there's a plan—and then the next your hope is all gone. I found myself trying to find comfort in poems and prayers. One about a child guardian angel I kept close by and recited over and over again.

LAURA: Oh, Mom. Go on.

DIANE: After your sister's death, I felt so much guilt. I felt guilt for not being there when she had that accident, for having a nanny who was too young and not watching closely enough. I found it hard to trust God. I trusted just enough to fight for you, hoping for another daughter, and here you are! That was faith. But so many people I loved have died: my ex-fiancé Dr. Terry, friends: Joan Shawlee, Shelley Winters, Helen Thomas, Joe Bologna, Harry Dean Stanton, Marlon Brando, and so many others. But your sister...

LAURA: Oh God, Mom. How you survived that I don't know.

DIANE: Fifty-two years I held this in my lungs—grief. Maybe that's part of why my lungs are hurting now. I held it in, just held it in, and now it's hard to get it out. When a child dies, there is a spiritual cord that breaks. It is so shocking physically and emotionally. It rips through your body. And your father emotionally ran away from himself—desperately. He couldn't face it, and so then he ran away from us. If you lose a child, it's very hard to cope. We were struggling actors. We could hardly make it. We had to stay in the same house where she died because we couldn't afford to leave. His family could have helped us, but they didn't.

LAURA: Oh, Mom. I'm so sorry.

DIANE: Children are not supposed to die before a parent. The pain is indescribable. The pain is too raw, it never leaves you. It's the real reason why your father and I split up. We were torn asunder. The neighbors brought pie and cake, and that was so kind, and some friends were there for us, not that any kindness could make us feel whole again. It felt like having our hair pulled out by the roots. How do you pick yourself back up after that? It shattered us. And the years that followed were bad in every way. The first time I got pregnant again, I had a tubular pregnancy and almost died. We couldn't get out of debt. We had no time, compassion, peace, harmony. It was horror after horror. How the hell are you going to survive that? This town doesn't respect suffering. Your father and I were a mirror of each other's pain at that time. If you have money, you can pull the shades down and help keep the ugliness out. Sometimes

In my grief — a poem that touched
my heart in, "Your Little Guardian Angel."
in which the first four lines read,

"Your little guardian angel, I am, my place is
an angel in a secret land.
I wasn't meant to live on earth just
touch your hand.
I've been sent to touch your lives and
I know you'll think that cruel,
but it's only special people that are
chosen exceptions to the rules...."

—*excerpt from* LITTLE ANGEL UNKNOWN *by* RONNIE HUNTER
modified by FRANCIE RUNMARK

people can make it through a tragedy easier when they have resources. You can hire people to help organize and plan.

LAURA: Dad told me that when he heard what had happened, James Whitmore immediately called and offered you and Dad work. Didn't say anything. Just put you to work. Is that true? He got you both jobs and got you paid and occupied.

DIANE: Yes, and we didn't even know him. Also, Tom called right away. One night he took us to the theater.

LAURA: By Tom, you mean Tennessee?

DIANE: Yes, he had a play opening, and he took us to that and to dinner, your father and me.

LAURA: Did he ever talk to you about grief or what you'd been through?

DIANE: No, he didn't have to. He already knew how we felt. He'd felt those feelings himself. He said we didn't have to talk, that we could just be together.

LAURA: I never heard that story. I find that so moving, that he was just silently there for you. He just said, "I'm scooping you up. We're going to the theater. And we're going to talk about art and have dinner after and just make it a beautiful night together."

DIANE: Yes, he took us to the theater, a place of healing for all of us. That meant so much, especially because some people in the family, especially in your father's family, were downright cold and didn't offer us any help at all. So you were asking about our divorce before, and that to me was the real reason for it, more than the cheating or any of the rest. I didn't know how to deal with the pain, and your father did not know how to handle the death of your sister. He just withdrew. It always seemed to me that he didn't relax with you until you were a day older than little Diane when she died.

LAURA: I guess I was the replacement child. I felt a responsibility to you and Dad and Grandma, to try to make sure you didn't have to feel that pain again. I think I grew up with a lot of anxiety. I worried about you guys.

DIANE: Laura! You were *not* a replacement. I know you think that we saw you that way, but we did not. I am grateful that I had your sister for the two years of her life before she was taken away. Thank God I got to have her in my arms. She was like you. At eighteen months, she was beautiful. Y'all were both brilliant.

LAURA: Oh, Mom. I'm so sorry.

DIANE: I can't look at this house without thinking of the end of my marriage.

LAURA: How exactly did it end? Was there one moment?

DIANE: I was up there this one day writing away when my little voice said, "You want to know what Bruce is doing? He's on the phone with another woman!" So help me God, I walked down those stairs and I picked up the other phone. I heard a girl giggling with him.

LAURA: Uh-oh.

DIANE: Bruce must've heard the phone click. I heard him say, "Wait a minute. Diane, Diane, honey?" I asked in a shaking voice, "Who is this?" The girl gasped and hung up.

LAURA: Oof.

DIANE: Bruce walked into the room where I was holding the receiver, and I said, "Bruce, that's a wrap!" For me, that moment was the end of our marriage, the last straw. Some people never divorce. I had hoped to be one of those people. But I just couldn't take it anymore. I went out and got in the car, and he ran after me, and he jumped in the car too. I said, "It just so happens I have an appointment with my therapist right now—and I sure need him!" He jumped in the car and went with me. Bruce tried to do his number for my therapist, but my therapist was not having it. At one point, I'm not even kidding, he grabbed your father by the neck and pushed him against the wall.

LAURA: Your *therapist*? No, he did not!

DIANE: I swear to God he did. And he said, "Boy, this is not your mother! This is your wife!" That was it. I was done. He had given me my children. I had loved him. He was a great lover in his own way, your dad. For a moment in time, I couldn't even hate him. I was numb. Burned. Ash bound.

LAURA: Mom!

DIANE: I think your father and I could have stayed married if we'd been more evolved. We could have had a great life. We're still friends and work great together.

LAURA: How did you deal with the breakup?

DIANE: I remember I went out and bought him a beautiful blue suit—maybe, unconsciously, so he could find love again. I didn't want him to mourn for me. You've just got to let go. If somebody wants to move on, you need to let them. Remember what Reese says to you whenever a man isn't treating you right? "Dern, you're prime real estate!" She is right. You have to remember that about yourself! If he doesn't see it, move on. And that's what I told myself.

LAURA: Mom, come on! This is me you're talking to. You don't need to put on a show of independence. The story doesn't even make sense. He cheated on you, so you bought him a suit and gave him your blessing? No way. I'm not buying it. I've been through a divorce. A lot of my friends have been through divorces. I know that's never how it goes. Tell me. What did you *really* do?

DIANE: Well, I did really buy him a suit, Laura! I wanted to take the high ground. But fine. I was also jealous. And one time I went after that girl he'd been talking to with my high heel. I tried to take her eyes out. Thank goodness someone held me back.

LAURA: And there it is. Thank you! I think that's a little more relatable. Breathe. You know, I can't believe this was our home.

DIANE: I'm getting cold.

LAURA: Here, Mom, take my jacket too. That shawl isn't enough.

DIANE: No, you'll get a chill.

LAURA: I'm fine. Let's just stand here and check your oxygen. It's reading eighty-nine.

DIANE: Uh-oh. They say under ninety and I'm supposed to use my oxygen tank.

LAURA: OK. First let's just stand in front of this beautiful spot and breathe. Trust me. Just close your eyes. Think about being in that home, and think about the fact that you chose to put your faith in my father, which is a gorgeous act of love. You can't control what he does with it, but you got your children from that trust and faith, and you built a family. Just like Dad always tells me: "Diane and I will be great loves for the rest of our life, because we made you."

DIANE: Let's go.

LAURA: Mom, first, please try, instead of first thinking about that home as *I had a divorce in that house,* maybe think, *I became a mother in that home,* or *I rebuilt my life in that home.*

[Silence.]

LAURA: *[continuing]* And Mom, after you split up he moved out into the apartment building at the end of the block to stay close...

DIANE: I did get through it. Her life was a gift to me. I realized finally that her death had cracked me open like a walnut to get out the sweet meat of my soul. Then, I wanted to be pregnant again, so desperately, but when I did it was a tubular pregnancy and I almost died. Then I prayed and studied about things that could help my body—the doctor said I could never have another child. So I prayed and God answered my prayer—or you did—because you chose me and He gave you to me.

LAURA: You want your oxygen?

DIANE: No, I'm fine now.

LAURA: Yeah, you are. I'll go get the car.

"You know, I was thinking this morning as I waited for you that it's very hard to see the truth, or to see the sun when it's hidden behind a cloud. And you help me try to remove the cloud, to let the sun shine on us."

—LAURA

MY PHOTO OF LAURA ON HER FIRST TRIP TO PARIS

Diane

After yesterday's walk, I feel lighter. I went home and fell into my first deep sleep in a long time. I woke up feeling five years younger. After this conversation, I felt understanding and peace of mind. I still felt tremendous sadness and regret over Diane Elizabeth's death. But I also felt a new feeling: pride that I'd gone on with my life and had not succumbed to grief. Laura gave me that forgiveness. She said, "Look what you've accomplished!" She took an arrow of pain and pulled it out of me. She did that standing there before me on the sidewalk. I'd avoided that block for a long time. She pushed me to go there, and as we talked in front of the old house, the layers of the past fell off like the layers of an onion. With nothing more than her love and her wisdom. I could see, finally, that yes, after surviving the unimaginable, I did OK. Life slapped me against the wall, but I came back. I worked, I had this beautiful second child. I have grandchildren. Laura taught me today that the wind blows, but eventually you see the sun again. You see that you have a treasure standing there next to you.

WALK

15

WHAT WE
LEAVE BEHIND

DIANE: Our last walk for a while! You were right about them writing my cannula into *Chesapeake Shores* if I need it, bless them. And there's a temporary ban, for starters, on the spraying of glyphosates!

LAURA: Yes, I'm so glad. You should be so proud of what you've accomplished for the health of that part of the country—and for your ability to work again too. And you're so strong now I can barely keep up with you. This walking-and-talking thing worked, didn't it?

DIANE: Yes, it worked. Our talking and your love have prolonged my life, I just know it. They said I'd be dead in six months. Instead, here we are months beyond that, and I'm so much stronger. It makes me angry on behalf of people who hear "throw in the towel" diagnoses and don't have someone like you to nurse them back to health or resources to fight. It's heartbreaking to me. Doctors should never write off a patient. It's like my father said: "You don't ever give *up* on life, as long as you are *in* life." And now that I'm well enough, I get to work again.

LAURA: And I'm going to go get Ellery ready for college. Mom, it's really freaking me out! Jaya said, "You better get used to it. I'm gone in like a year and a half." I was like, "Jaya, slow down; you're in eighth grade."

DIANE: Oh, honey. That's a sign that you did a good job with your kids. They feel secure, and they're ready to make their own way. And it's time now for them to be out in the world. I see so much brilliance in them, and their passion has not yet been freed. It's time for them to figure out what they want to do in the world and to go out and do it. They have a beautiful foundation, more in terms of education and love than I was even able to give you. Here's a question: If, God forbid, your life ended now, what would you want your legacy to be?

LAURA: Listen to you, asking the tough questions now! We've come a long way on these walks, haven't we?

DIANE: Yes! I learned from you! And the legacy question is something I think about so much, because when you're in your eighties, you feel you have to remind everyone of anything you ever did. People forget so quickly. I've been in over sixty feature films and a hundred and fifty-seven TV shows. I've gotten a crack at a truly great part approximately every eight years! Fifty years, with some truly special roles— *The Wild Angels, Alice Doesn't Live Here Anymore, Wild at Heart, Rambling Rose, The Cemetery Club, Joy, The Last Full Measure, Gigi & Nate,* and just now *Isle of Hope*...I've been nominated *three* times for an Oscar and won some seventy awards for my country, including the British academy award over Ingrid Bergman—*not* chopped liver! God gave me talent and I worked hard, but I'm a lucky duck! That's why I'm a SAG board member for thirty years. I'm fighting to pay it forward for those not as lucky. I have done all this work and must not, cannot let it die. I also think I need to stay present for my grandchildren. But really my main legacy is you, Laura. Your gifts are enormous, and you're the best thing I gave the world.

LAURA: Aw, Mom. Well, I've been reflecting on Jaya's and Ellery's childhoods, thinking through the mistakes I made and the painful moments that they experienced. I can't help thinking, *Shit, that was it! That was my opportunity to shape them as people. The childhood experience they had is what it's going to be.* Feeling that way has been really hard. So I've been thinking a lot about being a mother. What have I given my children to set them on their way? But because of what you and I have been through this year, I found myself comforted. It's not the truth that I'm done as a mother. Parents continue to support and shape their children forever. Our relationship, you and me, didn't stop when I moved out. If anything, we're closer now than we've ever been.

DIANE: You betcha. The other day I thought, *Ellery must be having a good time because he's not calling me much right now.* I could have nagged him, but then I thought about you and me, and I thought, *Let the bird fly.* I think about you, precious, and I see you as a baby. In my mind, I'm holding you in my arms. And I start to think, *Did I love her enough? Did I kiss her enough? Did I hug her enough?* I wish I could do it all over again. But then I see us here on these walks, and I think, *It will never be enough.* I will always want to love you more, to kiss you more.

LAURA: I think every parent on Earth knows that longing.

DIANE: You know what I just realized? If I live ten more years, to ninety-five, then Ellery would be twenty-nine. Then if I live to be a hundred, Ellery would be thirty-five. He might be married and have a baby by then. Maybe I will get to rock my great-grandbaby!

LAURA: The way Grandma Mary got to rock him.

DIANE: Oh my heavens, remember that? Sitting in that rocking chair at your house in the Hollywood Hills.

LAURA: What a feeling that must be, to hold your great-grandchildren.

DIANE: That was an amazing day. Grandma Mary sat there with this expression as if she'd seen God, holding Ellery for hours. I'll never forget it. She looked as if her whole life was flashing in front of her.

LAURA: I felt so close to you when I was alone in the middle of the night holding my baby and realizing, *Wow, my mother did this with me. I bet she felt this same feeling of boundless love.* Isn't it crazy that I didn't say that to you then? That I didn't share that on the days when my children were born, how close I felt to you? Mom, this whole experience, these walks—they've meant so much. I had thought, knowing what a storyteller you are, that I could keep you going by getting you to answer questions while I listened. But I didn't know what this time would give me. I used to believe in leaving things unspoken, trusting that in their hearts people knew the truth. I thought to feel love was enough. But this experience has changed that. I want you to hear it, to know what I feel. Still, some things I find it hard to speak aloud. So I wanted to give you this letter.

DIANE: Thank you. I am excited to read it. Now let's go home. Not because I'm tired, but because I have work to do. And don't you worry about letting your children go into the world. Look at us. Look at how happy I am. I'm with my daughter in the sunshine. Let them fly. You'll find each other again.

Laura

Dear Mom,

How do I share all that you mean to me? How do I express all that I admire and love? I feel that in childhood I always let you know how much you mattered. But then the resentful teenage years came in, where I needed autonomy and to break free from you. Then in adulthood I spent so much time trying to discover who I was that I let a distance come between us—mostly so I could learn to fall without you always picking me up.

I was so filled today with all that I appreciate about you that I started to write down these thoughts, as though again they were for me to keep locked away in a journal. Then I remembered all that you've opened me up to through these walks, the importance of sharing what I feel and what you mean to me. So here goes.

I've never seen someone love more fully than you love. You love Shakespeare as passionately as Law and Order: SVU. You always cuddle me the minute you see me, unless I have a dessert you want—then you hunt me down.

You turn heartbreak into hilarity. You make the most expressive sounds I've ever heard when it comes to your enjoyment of good food or a great movie. You have redone your Rolodex twenty-six times—that I know of. You love to write—all night, most nights. Unless you see what's on TV and get swept up into watching Fred Astaire and Ginger Rogers in Swing Time.

You love buttermilk, especially if you can soak a biscuit in it. You always eat black-eyed peas on New Year's. You will never say no to a loved one in need, even an ex. You used to pretend you were born in France because you wanted to be Simone Signoret. You love to go on cleansing fasts and then break them with a piece of pecan pie and a scotch and soda. And as we've said before, you love dreaming big, and you never give up on your dreams. But mostly, Mom, with all that I admire about you, and with all your qualities that make me laugh out loud, it's deep empathy that's your superpower. You will always fight for the needs and rights of a stranger on the street. That has been your greatest influence on me, and it's the trait I most hope to pass along to my own children.

We took these walks for your sake. That's what I told myself. But now I see that these walks were as much for me as they were for you. If this was our Arabian Nights, we're both Scheherazade. The hero's journey is never the journey we expect—that of teaching others to see themselves. It's the journey of being vulnerable enough to see oneself.

Thanks to you, I no longer have the same fears around aging and dying. I have learned that when I'm at my weakest and want to shut myself away, I should follow your example and lean into my family, lean into love. If not for you, I would have thought I should spare them, should slink away and hide. Now I know that it is not a burden to be with someone who loves you when you are suffering. It is a gift.

Thank you for sharing your life with me. Thank you for sharing all you've walked through. And thank you for sharing your relationship with your own mother. Your honesty about that complicated and beautiful relationship gave me more room to honor the truth of ours.

This experience makes me want to tell everyone, whether they are a parent or a child or both: Talk more. Share your fear with your loved ones. Let them tell you their stories. It won't always be easy. Some days you will just be in each other's company, and little might be said, and you won't know what is being accomplished. But then, suddenly, you'll realize that you've grown closer. You've discovered something key about your family.

Because of your example, Mom, I know the kind of openness I'd like to have with my kids—in the living, in the aging, and even in the dying. And because of this, I believe, this is how Ellery and Jaya will communicate with their children. Your courage will reverberate through our family for generations.

Your willingness to share your weakness strengthened me as I watched it strengthen you. What an unparalleled gift. Thank you, Mom. Thank you for walking and talking with me.

Love,
Laura

JAYA, DIANE, ELLERY, LAURA—ELLERY'S 21ST

QUESTIONS TO ASK ON YOUR OWN WALKS

What are the most powerful memories you have of childhood?

What or who were your first and most important influences?

What are your favorite things—song, movie, book, food?

What do you regret, and of what are you most proud?

Whom would you like to forgive or be forgiven by?

Who were the loves of your life? What were the heartbreaks?

What gives your life meaning? What do you want your legacy to be?

DIANE'S ACKNOWLEDGMENTS

I owe a "Thank You" to my Creator for the 'Opportunity of Life' and to my husband, Robert, and my daughter Laura, for their faith: even though doctors said, *"Only six months left to live,"* after I unknowingly absorbed Poisonous Pesticide chemicals in 2018. They inspired me to continue on fulfilling my Destiny with joy and love for the 'Highest Good.' My first miracle, after the tragic death of my two-year-old daughter, I experienced a Tubular Pregnancy, and the doctors said, *"You will never have another child; it is impossible."* I replied, "I will." And I did! Laura Dern is my first miracle. Recovering my own life is my second miracle.

Gracious ones who helped me feel the energy to live: in alphabetical order, Steve Anderson, Wendell Bachman, Laurel Felice, June Field, Mary Jo Healy, Nirmala Heriza, Lynn Kaplan, Todd Risley, Shirley Smith, Kim Vincent, Howard Wills, and Candace Wilson. Agent: Aron Gianini. Agent: Mollie Glick. Former Agent/Manager: Iris Grossman. Attorney: Stephen Breimer. Attorney: Patricia Glaser. Attorney: Jason Aylesworth. Doctors: Rachael Beller, Mark Berman, Robin Bernhoft, Kenneth Chang, Pradip Doshi, Dominique Fradin-Read, and Nurse Charles, Phillip Fleshner, Harris Gelberg, Richard Horowitz, Ken Kafka, Arthur and Carol Kornhaber, Jeff Kupperman, Nikhil Kumta, Gladys T. McGarey, Doug Nelson and wife Donna, and Nurse Gail, Cynthia Watson, and Nurse Linda. UCLA Medical Plaza: Dr. Eric Esrailian, Teresa Moussa, and Harry Solorzano; Todd Bates; Majda Benkhadra; Dr. John Belperio; Diana Son. Jacinte Paquette and Staff. Former manager Stephany Hurkos and family. Former manager Scott Hart. Business manager: Philpott Meeks and David Butler/Karine/Sandy/Harry/Victor/Elija/Cathy and all.

Animal Trainer Tracy Kelley who saved my "Murray," and Dog Walker Tony Sabala, who took care of my treasured pets when I could not be there. Stand-in: Iona Kaye. Writing partners: Carlton Scott Alsop, William Jack Sibley. Actors Studio East: Deborah Dixon. Actors Studio West: Helen Sanders, et al. Directors: Martha Coolidge, Roger Corman, James Dearden, Jonathan Demme, Roger Donaldson, Bill Duke, Nick Hamm, Todd Haynes, Tonya Holly, Demian Lichtenstein, David Lynch, Todd Robinson, Damian Romay, David O. Russell, Martin Scorsese, Harry Winer, among others. Assistants: Michelle Pauley, Katya Priestley, Sylvia Hague, and former assistant and "adopted" daughter Brittany B. Fowler. My very talented other "son," Damien Chazelle.

Aunt: Johni B. DuBose and daughters. Cousins: Lahoma DuBrock, Alene Ladner, Debra Ladner Fink, Amy Lanier, Irma Jean Kirkland, Fred Newman, Kathy and Marvin Strahan. My ex- husbands Bruce Dern and William Shay Jr.

Friends: My "adopted family" (alphabetical order) Ellen Elliott-Applegate, Fern Barishman, Dr. Harvey Bank, Bonnie Birch and family, Beth Brickell, Gael Belden, Bradley Cooper and mother Gloria, Glenda Christian and Bill Young, Colleen Camp, Jody Carter, Heather Collins and family, Joe D'Angerio, Connie DeNave, Robert Duval, Francis Fisher, Jane Fonda, Elliot Gould, Debi Otto and Ray Harding, Lainie Kazan and daughter Jennifer and family, Sally Kirkland, Shery Lund and family, Ron Jackson, Jay Jennings, Sharon and Bob Jiminez, Sandra Martin, Stephanie and Linda Matlow, Mary McLaglen, Kathy Mitchell, Barbara Niven and Chesapeake bunch, Patty Pagaling, Evangeline Rogers, Nancy Sinatra, Donna and Steve Sallen, Connie Stevens and Joely and Tricia, Tamara Trexler, Renee Taylor and son Gabe Bologna, Rebecca and Josh Tickell, Emily Tracy and Bertold Haas, Lucas and Nicki and Simon, Michelle Vicary, Brenda Vaccaro, Marianne Williamson, and Bonnie White. Mentored brilliant actress: Sarina Freda.

My beloved grandchildren: C. J. Harper, Harris Harper, Ellery W. Harper, Jaya E. Harper. My ex-son-in-law by marriage Ben Harper. My son-by-marriage Brandon and wife Kristen and Aiden and Avery. Daughter-by-Amy Hunter Oleson and Rylie and Madilyn. Daughter-by-marriage Emily Hunter Ragsdale and husband Jason and sons Travis and Houston with their always loving notes. Like family: Kristy West-brook and husband Michael and family. Godchild: Bellina Logan and husband Ben Bode and daughter Lola.

My family, friends, teachers, and guides on the other side of the Veil: Thank you for "being" you. All my gratitude to Suzanne O'Neill and the Grand Central Publishing staff. And, last but not least, my "other daughter." Reese Witherspoon—thank you for the introduction, darling.

Much love in light,

Diane

LAURA'S ACKNOWLEDGMENTS

Thank you to my mother for your bravery and determination and for your willingness to believe . . . to have faith in your own healing beyond diagnoses, and for trusting me enough to take these walks together. Also, thank you for your stories and your unconditional love.

I am grateful to Mom for mentioning our amazing doctors who believed in her ability to heal—and who keep fighting and searching for alternative cures for lesser understood health crises—particularly Dr. Dominique Fradin-Read and Dr. Cynthia Watson.

Thank you to my children, my great gift in this life. Thank you for countless hours of love and support to your nana; for having guitar lessons at her apartment, for dinners, and for showing her so much love at such a fractured time. I love you, amazing Jaya and Ellery. And thank you to my incredible stepchildren, CJ and Harris, for your unwavering support and love and endless kindness. How exciting to be inspired daily by the four of you as I watch your art and your humanity grow.

To my father, Bruce—thank you for your inspiration, your authenticity, your irreverence, your stories, and your genes. I love you with all my heart.

Thank you to all our extraordinary climate change activists and environmental heroes: Ken Cook and the Environmental Working Group; Rebecca and Josh Tickell; Heather Collins, Tim, and the boys, the best neighbors and protectors on the planet. Daniel Hinerfeld and the NRDC; Oceana; Greenpeace; Monica Ramirez, civil rights attorney for Justice for Migrant Women, and friend. First Partner of California, Jen Siebel Newsom; Adam Vega; America's Food Fund and to all those who fight to move us from industrialized farming to regenerative farming and protect us from the use of petrochemicals, pesticides, and GMOs.

To Robert Hunter, for standing beside Mom with your love, dedication, and determination for her healing and her happiness.

To my incredible friends who showed up at this time to offer my mother so much love and support as she attempted to rebuild:

My sister Bellina, brother Ben Bode, and niece Lola Bode; amazing Jill and Ed Vedder, who did everything from decorating a Santa Monica apartment to coming up with the title of this book.

To my sister and my heart Reese Witherspoon, thank you for your gorgeous foreword, for Grandma Betty, and for knowing and loving your family; Jayme and Fritz Lemons, loyal, loving, consistent family forever; Frida Aradottir for love, sisterhood, and making mom feel pretty; Courteney Cox and Coco Arquette, for making me, Nana, and the kids your family; Nicole Avant and Ted Sarandos for being my angels, champions, and for loving the binder. Marianne Williamson, for all your love and prayer; Gloria and Bradley Cooper for love, holidays, friendship, and even giving Nana a home; the Stevens girls—Connie, Joely, Trisha; Lanie Kazan; Henry Bildstein, who would take on no job too little to support my parents; Kaiman Kazazian; cake taker and buddy to us all; for Mandy Foreman (my Penny); Stephanie and Linda Matlow for endless love, food, and spend the nights; cousin Deborah Fink; Dalia Rota (my Lala); Cleo Wade and Simon Kinberg for Ojai trips and loving Diane's stories; Irena and Mike Medavoy for always checking in and giving love; Jean-Marc Vallée for your love, art, and sending Mom flowers; Isabella Rossellini, for caring for my mother like she's yours; David Lynch for constant love and being my family and my maestro; Mary Steenburgen and Ted Danson for offering love, food to Mom, and being the best godparents to my children; sister Cecilia and Daniel Peck Voll; Nina Amadeus; Keiko Matsuo; Lisa Sutton and Amy Lafayette, acupuncture goddesses; Raf Simons, for paying tribute to Mom!; and Thurn Hoffman, researcher, brother, and angel.

Thank you, family members Peter Levine, Mollie Glick, and CAA, for your profound advocacy and love on this. Thanks to Simon Green for your inspiration and guidance. Annett Wolf, my sister, thank you for your partnership and loyalty all these years. Thank you, Jason Weinberg, for your tireless support and love. Thank you, Mike Rosenfeld and Charlie Jennings, for your representation and care. Thank you, Mara Hofman, Stacy Sealock, and HCVT for your patience, support, and constant guidance. Thank you, Chris Hyacinthe, for endless hours of editing, support, transcripts, tip-ins, photo approvals, and food treats for being a constant calm in any storm. To Mom's assistants, Brittany, Katja, and Michelle—thank you for your unwavering support for Mom and our book. Thank you, Flea, for your brilliant support, advice, and inspiration. Thank you to Jona Frank for your brilliant photographs and your love. To Gabriele Wilson for your tireless artistic efforts and to everyone at Grand Central for helping us fulfill this dream.

Thank you to my found family. Whether it be through childhood or art as a daughter, mother, or friend, you have guided me, influenced, or supported me on this journey.

Thank you to my sisters (alphabetized by last name):

Laura Alvarez; Rosanna Arquette; my BLL sisters—Nicole Kidman, Zoe Kravitz, Meryl Streep, Reese Witherspoon, Shailene Woodley; Cate Blanchett; Kate Capshaw; Joyce Chopra; Imelda Colindres, my sister, my nanny, my home; Martha Coolidge; Sheryl Crow; Greta Gerwig; Pam Goldblum; Amy Griffin; Judy Hofflund; Greta Kaufman; Diane Lane; Marbelly Morales, nanny and family; Stella McCartney; Julianne Moore; Jessie Nelson; Mary Kay Place; Alex Rockwell; Meg Ryan; Brooke Shields; hero Cheryl Strayed; Frances Tamaariki; Christine Taylor; Angie Toops; Phoebe Waller-Bridge; Naomi Watts; Moon Zappa.

And other members of my found family (alphabetized by last name):

Scott Alsop; Noah Baumbach; Emily and Berthold Haas and Lukas, Niki, and Simon Haas; Bekah Bourget; Laura Brown; Carol Burnett; Maha Dakhil; Alex Derbyshire; Andrea Dern; Tallulah de Saint Phalle; Clare Dingle; Peggy Feury; Laurence Frauman; Jonathan Gale; Andrew Garfield; Doris Kearns Goodwin; Bryan Gordon and Molly Gordon; John Griffin; Marcia Gay Harden; Ben Harper (thank you for our amazing children); Joanna Harper; Woody and Laura Harrelson; Roda and Tor Hermansen; Michael Kovac and Karina Maher; Lyn and Norman Lear; Brian Lindstrom; Kathy Kennedy and Frank Marshall; Sam Neill; Mimi Novak; Guy Oseary and Michelle; Alexander Payne and Peggy Payne; Samantha Power and Cass Sunstein; Jay Roach and Susanna Hoffs; Tracy Roberts; David O. Russell; Steven Spielberg; Lee Strasberg; Mike White.

Guardian angels:

Averil Logan, Veronique Peck, Kelly Preston, Jean-Marc Vallée, Betty (Bellina's nanny), Jonathan Demme, Peter Bogdanovich, Jacqueline Avant, Natasha Richardson, Tom Cole, Joan Shawlee, Jim Glennon, Jamal, Buddy Love, Shelley Winters.

LAURA AND SANDRA

And to you, Grandma Mary—my heart, my guide, my everything.

And to my other mama, my muse in the art of healing and acting. My north star. My beloved teacher, Sandra Seacat.

A wise man who lives on Oahu reminded me, "Live every day like it's a memory you've chosen to revisit."

I thank all of you named above and so, so many more, who have inspired me to want to live by the above motto—from the people and the animals I've been privileged to love, to great cinema, to *I Love Lucy*, to peach cobbler... I am excited to revisit with you all soon.

IMAGE CREDITS

Unless otherwise credited, all photos are courtesy of the authors.

Interior

p. 10: Pictorial Press Ltd/Alamy Stock Photo

p. 16: Cinematic Collection/Alamy Stock Photo

p. 17: Album/Alamy Stock Photo

p. 41: MediaPunch Inc/Alamy Stock Photo

p. 58: Bettmann/Contributor/Getty Image

p. 72: I. Glory/Alamy Stock Photo

p. 93: Paramount/Kobal/Shutterstock

p. 94: American International Pictures/Handout/Getty Image

p. 103: Everett Collection, Inc./Alamy Stock Photo

p. 104: Album/Alamy Stock Photo

p. 151: colaimages/Alamy Stock Photo

p. 151: Silver Screen Collection/Contributor/Getty Image

p. 151: Silver Screen Collection/Contributor/Getty Image

p. 151: Silver Screen Collection/Contributor/Getty Image

p. 151: Print Collector/Contributor/Getty Image

p. 151: Bettmann/Contributor/Getty Image

p. 151: ullstein bild Dtl./Contributor/Getty Image

p. 152: © Jona Frank

p. 152: © Jona Frank

p. 159: ©1994 Showtime Networks Inc., a Paramount Company. SHOWTIME and related marks are trademarks of Showtime Networks Inc. Mrs. Munck © Showtime Networks Inc. All Rights Reserved.

p. 190: Zoonar GmbH/Alamy Stock Photo

p. 204: © Jona Frank

p. 235: © Jona Frank

Insert

Laura, Grandma Mary, and Diane: © Jayne Wexler

Diane and Laura on a bench: © Jona Frank

WALKING AND TALKING, THE BLUFFS, SANTA MONICA, CA

ABOUT THE AUTHORS

LAURA DERN is an award-winning actress, producer, creator, and activist. She has received a number of accolades, including an Academy Award, an Emmy, and five Golden Globe Awards. Dern is also a passionate environmentalist.

DIANE LADD is an international award-winning actress, receiving a BAFTA Award, a Golden Globe Award, and Women of the Year award. She is a three-time Oscar and three-time Emmy nominee, having appeared in more than 187 films and television shows. She is a director, writer, producer, and author with degrees in esoteric psychology/nutrition, a lifetime member of the Actors Studio, and on the National Board of Directors for SAG/AFTRA.